Architecture in Old Chicago

Architecture in Old Chicago

THOMAS E. TALLMADGE

THE UNIVERSITY OF CHICAGO PRESS

CHICAGO · LONDON

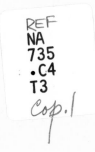
THE UNIVERSITY OF CHICAGO PRESS, CHICAGO 60637
THE UNIVERSITY OF CHICAGO PRESS, LTD., LONDON

International Standard Book Number: 0-226-78947-0

Table of Contents

Introduction vii

Prefatory Note xv

I. THE BIRTH OF A CITY 1

II. CHILDHOOD, 1830-1855 27

III. GROWING PAINS, 1855-1880 64

IV. ROMANCE, 1880-1893 133

INDEX 209

Introduction

*A*rchitecture in Old Chicago is the valedictory of a
long and distinguished career in the practice and interpretation of a great art. Its posthumous publication will
carry emotional overtones to the author's nation-wide
circle of friends and associates, and the many readers of
his *Story of Architecture in America* and *Story of England's Architecture* will, no doubt, place it upon a book-
shelf beside those larger works with a sense of loss, for
in them they had found a writer who brought a high
degree of charm, and even humor, to the treatment of
a technical subject.

Yet this work was not intended by Thomas Eddy
Tallmadge to be his last word. His years were ripening,
but he remained young in spirit. There was much of the
eternal boy in him, and he always looked forward to
new adventures of the mind. *Architecture in Old Chicago*
was not planned as an archaeological study, but as the
history of his city in terms of architecture from the palisades of a military post in a wilderness to the soaring
towers of the present. He had brought his story up to
Chicago's conquest of international fame with the Columbian Exposition of 1893, or as the native-born say, "the
first World's Fair," when his career came to a sudden
and tragic end on January 1, 1940.

Nevertheless, the chapters that he had completed round out a cycle of the city's history, and have a unity in themselves. They deserve presentation as an organic work, and *Architecture in Old Chicago* cannot be taken as merely a fragment of an unfinished design. This book forms the complete record of study, meditation and research on a subject that the author probably stated to himself in these terms: "What was behind me, in the growth of this great city, when I, as a boy, first began to dream of adding to its church spires and its homes?"

A lifetime of field work has gone into this book. When I first met Tom Tallmadge, I discovered that he was a hunter and collector of dates on buildings, for they, when correlated with cornices, window trim and other technical details, had much to tell him about the rude forefathers of the hamlet. That was thirty years ago, and long before he had started his architectural writing. When I last saw him, shortly before his death, it was on a "house hunting" expedition for historical purposes, when I served as a Dr. Watson to his Sherlock Holmes.

The purpose of this introduction is chiefly biographical, and yet the necessary facts and dates, although they are numerous, will not give a satisfactory picture of the man. To say that he was born in Washington, D.C., in 1876 is unimportant; but to add that he belonged to Evanston, Chicago's largest and most famous suburb, is significant. There he was reared and schooled until the sense of a vocation took him to Massachusetts Institute of Technology. There he lived afterward; and there he built his first great church, which many consider his masterpiece; there was his home town of a lifetime. His studio on Pearson Street, in Chicago's Greenwich Village, was an important focus of his varied social activities and hobbies; the Cliff Dwellers Club, where a fine portrait of him by Edgar Miller may be seen, was another; and the Art Institute of Chicago, where he often lectured, was a shrine for his spirit. The office of Tallmadge and Watson, at Madison and Wells Streets, where more than 250 buildings grew from the drafting boards as the years passed by, was, of course, a necessary functional locale. But when the job was done, or the etching finished, or the party over, Tom Tallmadge rode the Elevated home to Evanston, and there, close to the shadow of his First Methodist church whose square tower marks the farthest north of Chicago's skyline, was his home.

Then there was the Summer School of Painting at Saugatuck, Michigan. For twenty-five years he was its tutelary genius, its patron, its feudal lord, and much of his time in the fair weather seasons was spent beside its oxbow lagoon and among its wooded dunes, amusing himself with etching or painting. Saugatuck, however, was not a workshop for him; it was his favorite playground. He was a Nature lover with a quiet passion for the out-of-doors, and Saugatuck was his isle of Innisfree. On his sylvan domain is a place that he called "the temple"—a natural amphitheater around which trees rise like columns; and there, if an initiate will lead you into the fastness, you will find a bronze memorial to him, placed by companions in the Saugatuck fellowship.

You will find keys to the unique personality of Tallmadge on the shores of Lake Zurich, Illinois, where he often week-ended in a hermitage that is part golf club and part farm; and along the canoeing routes of the Fox, Kankakee and Kalamazoo rivers; and in the duck-shooting blinds of the Bear River Gun Club near the Great Salt Lake in Utah. The poems of John Keats, which he could quote more copiously than the average professor of English, were also a part of him; and a pocket copy of the Oxford Book of English Verse, which he carried on every outing, bearing the stains of marsh water and fisherman's thumb-prints, would, if extant, evoke much of the man.

Tallmadge's feeling for Nature was deep-seated, and his scholarly trend of mind made him a first-rate amateur in several branches of the natural sciences. On a canoe trip from Allegan to Saugatuck down the Kalamazoo, through fairly wild country, he surprised me with his ability to name birds by their flight or call. I began to jot down the species he identified, and found that in a few hours the list ran to more than fifty. Astronomy was another of his mild hobbies, and thereby hangs a bit of architect's shop-talk. After a dinner party, he chatted with a fellow guest whom he had never met before and of whose profession he was ignorant. He pointed out some of the constellations in the summer sky, giving them their names, and his companion listened with interest. A few months later he received a letter from this chance acquaintance, stating that his taste for astronomy qualified him as the architect to build an observatory for Ohio Wesleyan University.

Tallmadge was graduated as bachelor of science in architecture at Massachusetts Institute of Technology in 1898. He immediately entered the office of Burnham and Root in Chicago as draftsman, and served with this firm for seven years. Among the Burnham and Root commissions of that period was Orchestra Hall in Chicago, in which there are some forgotten traces of his work.

In 1905 Tallmadge entered independent practice with Vernon S. Watson, another graduate from the drafting rooms of Burnham and Root. This partnership continued until 1934 and covered the major part of Tallmadge's career. His first commission of importance came in 1909, when planning began for the First Methodist Church of Evanston. (In 1930 he added to this impressive Gothic edifice its chapel and cloister, and also remodelled the auditorium.) This was a triumph for a young firm, and Tallmadge became marked as a specialist in ecclesiastical architecture. His larger commissions thereafter were chiefly in this field.

Among the other notable churches that Tallmadge designed are St. James' Methodist, at 46th Street and Ellis Avenue; the First Presbyterian, at 64th Street and Kimbark Avenue; Grace Episcopal, close to St. Luke's Hospital (all in Chicago); the First Congregational, in Evanston, and the Grace Evangelical Lutheran, in River Forest. A complete list of his churches would contain about twenty-five other names. Most of them are in Chicago and its suburbs, but good examples may also be found in Niles and Benton Harbor, Michigan, Elgin, Illinois, Hastings, Nebraska, and Neenah, Wisconsin.

His contributions to campus architecture were not numerous, although his gift for ecclesiastical design should have made him an adept in the style called collegiate Gothic. In addition to the Perkins Astronomical Observatory at Ohio Wesleyan, already mentioned, he designed the Wrenn Library at the University of Texas, Roycemore School, Evanston, and (with William N. Alderman, his associate from 1936 until his death) a men's dormitory at Ripon College.

Tallmadge's career as a writer on architectural subjects began in 1925. This was a natural development out of his frequent lectures in a popular vein at the Art Institute and his teaching in the architectural school of Armour Institute of Technology from 1906 until 1927. As an educator, his courses were in the field of architectural history.

His debut as a writer was made with an essay called

"The Advance of Architecture," published in the *Atlantic Monthly* in August, 1925. Its immediate acceptance was a complete surprise to him; he had not imagined that he was in the Atlantic class as a writer, and had submitted it to that magazine only at the suggestion of a friend who read the manuscript and found it a graceful treatment of a technical subject, with a definite literary value. This essay brought to Tallmadge four offers from publishers who believed that he was the man to write a popular history of American architecture. A few years before his death *The Advance of Architecture* was republished in a college textbook of modern essays.

In research his favorite field was early American architecture. He could discover traces of the influence of the Greek Revival, for which he had a special fancy, in ancient shacks that were merely a blight on the landscape to his colleagues. He contributed to architectural nomenclature the name and description of the Parvenu period, which before his time had been unrecognized and anonymous. I can name the very place and the time when the Parvenu period was born in Tallmadge's mind. It was in a canoe on the Fox River, somewhere between Wilmot, Wisconsin, and Hackberry Island of the Fox Lake marshes, in June, 1920.

His reputation as a savant in American building design brought him an appointment to the advisory board of architects for the reconstruction of Williamsburg, Virginia, now so famous as an objective for tourists. The Colonial Village at A Century of Progress exposition in Chicago, 1934, was an ephemeral expression of his mastery of this field. He served as a chairman of the Advisory Committee of the Illinois District, Historical American Buildings Survey, a federal project. He also was a member of the National Advisory Committee of the Survey.

City planning commissions and the numerous movements and causes that can lay claim to a free share of an architect's time found him always willing to co-operate. His was an exceptionally active and generous life; he was constantly occupied with non-remunerative matters, and was always industrious without seeming to be a drudge. The many friends of his hours of recreation never thought of him as an arduous toiler until he told of consulting a physician for a touch of nervous exhaustion, and of the advice for which he had paid a handsome fee: "Simplify your life."

It is fortunate that Tallmadge was a writer as well as a builder. To his own generation his books carry the full flavor of his many-faceted personality, and thus he who had much to give to the world is not altogether lost. Future generations, even when the stones and steel in which he wrought have gone the way of all architecture, will find literary value and technical instruction in his humanized, well-documented works in architectural history.

The publication of *Architecture in Old Chicago* has been sponsored and arranged by Joseph T. Ryerson, John A. Holabird, Charles West and Ralph Fletcher Seymour, friends of the author, who are confident that this work will prove to be a valuable addition to the literature of its subject.

CHARLES COLLINS

Prefatory Note

THE text of this volume is published with a minimum of change from the original draft of a manuscript found in Mr. Tallmadge's effects. The illustrations have been added. An effort has been made to select those pictures which it is believed would have been Mr. Tallmadge's choice.

The sponsors of this volume desire to express their gratitude to the Burnham Library of the Art Institute and to the Chicago Historical Society which have given valuable assistance in connection with the illustrations. The committee also wishes to acknowledge its indebtedness to Mr. Earl H. Reed who gave generously of his time in preparing the manuscript for the Press. Mr. Richard Schmidt was good enough to read the manuscript for the committee.

JOSEPH T. RYERSON
JOHN A. HOLABIRD
CHARLES WEST
RALPH FLETCHER SEYMOUR

CHAPTER I

The Birth of a City

FORT Dearborn was most certainly Chicago's first work worthy to be called Architecture. There were, we all know, two forts. The first, built in 1803, was burned in 1812. The second, built in 1816, endured in decrepit old age for many years until the last of its aged bones were quietly and, we hope, reverently laid away. The earlier fort was by all means the more famous. The claim of the first fort as Chicago's first architectural monument cannot be threatened by previous buildings in old "Chicago." It is true that other buildings were said to have existed, but one of these was legendary, one was totally unknown, and the others were too humble to be admitted into even so democratic a family circle as Architecture.

Aside from the Indian wigwam, the first recorded habitation of man was the hallowed hut of Père Jacques Marquette, in which he spent the winter of 1674-75.[1] He refers to it in his journal as *"une cabannez,"* which in the *patois* of the *coureurs de bois* might mean cabin or wigwam. We know that the Jesuit priest and his companions had no heavy tools; so it is pretty safe to assume that their *cabannez* was a hut of some kind, probably made of

[1] This was the missionary's second trip to Chicago. The first was in the fall of 1673 while returning via the Chicago Portage with Joliet after their rediscovery and exploration of the Mississippi.

upright poles sunk in the ground, chinked and plastered with moss and clay and roofed with other poles, over which was laid the sail-cloth and buffalo hides or bark, weighted down with boughs and perhaps sod. It probably had no windows, and the cold of winter was denied by a little door hung on hinges of rawhide. The smoke possibly escaped through a hole in the roof, wigwam fashion, but there is no good reason to agree with the historians that their quarters were miserable or barbarous or that it was "the customary Indian shelter or wigwam." They had knives and undoubtedly axes, plenty of material and unlimited time; so it is unreasonable to believe that civilized men would be willing under the circumstances to be unnecessarily uncomfortable. Whatever their quarters, it is a pleasure to know that the Indians were more than friendly and supplied them with the corn and the game, even to bison (which the priest termed "cattle"), with which the country abounded. With reverent gratitude these Indians took as their compensation the gospel and the benediction of Father Marquette.

The next five years of life for Chicago glowed with the name of René Robert Cavelier, Sieur de La Salle. The ambition of this indomitable explorer was to be the architect of an empire which should be more than an affair of sticks and stones. Chicago served but as a means of access to his Mississippian realm. His forts of Crèvecoeur and St. Louis (Starved Rock) lie beyond the limits of our story, and so do his vision and his failure.

Whether the mission established by Père Pierre Pinet some time during 1696 was at Chicago and whether it had a chapel or other buildings are moot questions. One authority[2] is convinced that the mission was at Grosse

[2] Frank R. Grover.

Pointe on the edge of the Skokie marsh, while another [3] believes it to have been near the mouth of the Chicago river.

Father Pinet's mission is even excelled in tenuity by the legend of a fort during the French occupation. If there was one, it existed in that mysterious century of oblivion that began with the withdrawal of the French in 1700. There was none in Chicago in 1715.[4] Pierre Charlevoix, a great romancer, neglected a golden opportunity to locate one there in 1721. None is mentioned in any account of the Fox wars in 1730, nor in the report of Bougainville in 1757. Joutel, who lived at Chicago during the winter of 1687 and the spring of 1688, mentioned no fort. La Salle, however, in 1683 spoke of a fort "built at Chicagou" by two of his men, and in 1693 mention was made of a fort at Chicagou, together with the name of its commander. And, more than all this, in the famous Treaty of Greenville, 1795, which established the location of the first Fort Dearborn, occur the words "at the mouth of the Chikago River . . . where a fort formerly stood." Quaife, our great authority on the old Northwest, very ingeniously explains the contradictions by saying that the so-called "fort" of La Salle, which his lieutenant Tonty never mentioned though often in Chicago, was a temporary stockade. Built by only two men, it couldn't have been very formidable.

The other mention of a fort, a real one this time, refers to Fort Miami at the mouth of the St. Joseph river, which by a curious mistake is shown by Father Hennepin to flow into the southwestern side of Lake Michigan instead of the southeastern. We can therefore rest assured that, real or ethereal, whatever it was, it wasn't Architecture.

[3] M. M. Quaife, *Chicago and the Old Northwest* (1913).
[4] *Ibid.*

The fort and the house alike of the pioneer were built of logs, and of log-building there were two distinct techniques. The first, or older, was called the "French method." It was exemplified in Chicago itself by the old Cahokia Court House. This exotic and pathetic little building stood at bay, so to speak, on the Wooded Island in Jackson Park. Having been yanked hither and yon, it was given one last journey back to its birthplace in Cahokia. As an example of Chicago architecture it has no place in this narrative, but it does furnish a good example of the "French method" in log-building. The logs were usually of modest diameters, sharpened at their nether extremities, and side by side driven several feet into the ground with sledge hammers. Their tops were sawed to a line and a horizontal timber called a plate, roughly squared, was spiked into their tops. On this rested the ends of the roof rafters and the ceiling joists. Except where built of stone, as Fort Chartres, the old French forts along the Illinois and Mississippi rivers were built of logs in this fashion, as Fort Crèvecoeur.

The technique of the American, however, was a very different thing. It was that which resulted in the familiar "log house" of our experience. Its difference was basic, for in the "American fashion" the logs were laid horizontally, one on top of another. To keep them from falling down, as they were too big to nail, they were locked at the corners. This was done in at least three different ways. In the simplest, *A*, the logs were not prepared, but were rolled into place, often with the bark on. At the ends a quarter of the diameter of each log was notched out on exactly opposite sides (as shown), when the four walls were built. Fitted into place the ends of the logs joined like interlocked fingers, only much better. While theoretically there would be no space between the logs, actually there were spaces, due to irregularities and differences in diameters. Hence the logs were "chinked" by ramming clay, straw, moss and, later, mortar into the cracks.

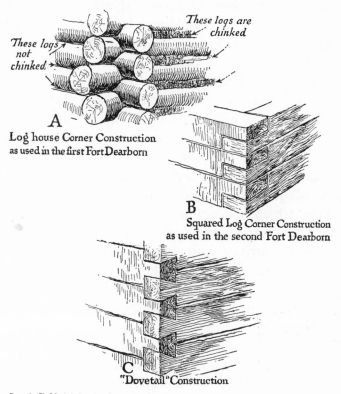

These logs are chinked

These logs not chinked

A

Log house Corner Construction as used in the first Fort Dearborn

B

Squared Log Corner Construction as used in the second Fort Dearborn

C

"Dovetail" Construction

Drawing by Ralph Fletcher Seymour

In the second and third methods, *B* and *C*, the logs were trimmed with an adz until they were practically square in section, and the ends were "halved," i.e., one-half of each was cut away. Here again the drawing is more eloquent than words. As far as method *C* is concerned, I defy anyone to explain a "dovetail" in words. The drawing expresses it better, though inadequately. Better still, examine the construction of your bureau drawer. If it is a good one, the front and sides will be "dovetailed" together. This last scheme was of course the strongest and involved the most work and the most skill.

Let Mrs. Kinzie (daughter-in-law of the John Kinzie who survived the Fort Dearborn Massacre) tell in *Wau-Bun* part of the story. "Building a log house is a somewhat curious process," she says. "The chimney is formed by four poles of the proper length, interlaced with a wicker-work of small branches. A hole or pit is dug near at hand, and with a mixture of clay and water a sort of mortar is formed. Large wisps of hay are filled with this thick substance and fashioned with the hands into what are technically called 'clay cats' and then are filled in among the framework of the chimney until not a chink is left. The whole is then covered with a smooth coating of the wet clay, which is denominated 'plastering.' Between the logs which compose the walls of the building small bits of wood are driven quite near together; this is called 'chinking,' and after it is done clay cats are introduced and smoothed over with the plaster. When all is dry, both walls and chimney are whitewashed and present a comfortable and tidy appearance. The roof is formed by laying upon the transverse logs thick sheets of bark, etc."

The first Fort Dearborn, as shown in the restoration at the Century of Progress, represented the first method of joining the logs. The second fort, as indicated by some of the logs preserved in the Chicago Historical Society, was an example of the second. The roof was covered with shingles, or shakes, split with an axe or "frow" from short sections of logs and nailed onto poles which ran parallel to the ridge. Where the conditions were so primitive that there were no nails the roof was probably covered with bark held in place with boughs, as the American pioneer never understood the English art of thatching, except in the crudest way. The log house usually had a gable at each end, which is curious, as a gable of logs is most insecure because the ends have no chance to interlock. Sometimes upright logs or slabs in the gables were used, a much

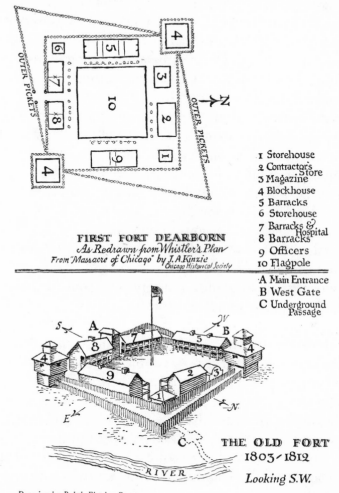

FIRST FORT DEARBORN
As Redrawn from Whistler's Plan
From "Massacre of Chicago" by J.A.Kinzie
Chicago Historical Society

1 Storehouse
2 Contractor's Store
3 Magazine
4 Blockhouse
5 Barracks
6 Storehouse
7 Barracks &.
8 Barracks Hospital
9 Officers
10 Flagpole

A Main Entrance
B West Gate
C Underground Passage

THE OLD FORT
1803–1812
Looking S.W.

Drawing by Ralph Fletcher Seymour

better method, but a hip roof, the most secure of all, was seldom used. The floor was usually of pounded clay, though as prosperity increased puncheons or heavy boards were often laid on top of the clay.

The door of hewn boards was hung in the earliest cabins on hinges of hide or of whittled ash or oak and the windows were filled with greased paper. What stone could be found was used for the hearth and fire-place, which connected with a chimney of wood heavily plastered with clay, as Mrs. Kinzie has described. The furniture was entirely home-made. Only firearms and kitchen utensils and bedding and children could pre-empt precious space on the back of horse or man.

When the sawmill arrived with its adjunct, the blacksmith shop, the log cabin took a step forward. Window-sash and glass filled the crude opening in the logs and wrought-iron hinges and nails secured flapping doors and shingles. As a matter of fact, the sawmill spelled the well-deserved doom of the log house.

There are several curious things about the log house. The first is that it was unknown among the seventeenth-century colonists. Pilgrims, Puritans and Cavaliers had never seen it in England, as there was none to see, and failed to invent it in a new world, obvious as it appears. The log house, as we know it, was probably introduced into Delaware by the Swedes not before 1720.[5] Another curious thing is that it is not a stable form of construction, sturdy and massive as it appears. There is always a basic inclination to roll over, restrained only by the ties at the log ends and weakened by every opening; and the logs, damp and unventilated, fall early victims to decay. There is probably not an eighteenth-century log house (built American-fashion) standing in the entire country. On account of the dampness of the logs, insects, etc., the pioneers said, "Lend your house to your enemy the first year, to your friend the second, and occupy it yourself the third."

[5] Fiske Kimball, *Domestic Architecture of the American Colonies and of the Early Republic*, pp. 7-8.

Next to the sawmill the greatest antagonist to the house of logs was the brick-kiln. It is erroneous to believe that bricks were late importations into the frontier. Bricks were a crying need for chimneys and fireplaces, were easy to make and required no especial apparatus. Very often the bricks were made on the premises, if of course clay was available. Brick and stone as well were used in Illinois before the construction of Fort Dearborn. Kaskaskia, founded in 1720, antedated Fort Dearborn by eighty-three years, and in its eighteenth-century buildings both brick and stone were common. And there was of course Fort Chartres, the greatest of all the French forts in the old Northwest, built mostly of stone, and cut stone at that, of which the ancient powder house still stands in mute evidence of departed might. In fact, in the earliest of the river towns both brick and stone were common, owing to the ease of flat-boat transportation and to the availability of material.

The forge and anvil of the blacksmith, though the last of the trinity to be mentioned here, were the first in chronological sequence. Rifles had to be kept in repair. After them nails and hardware had to be made for the cabin, shoes for the horses, tires for the wagons and, last of all, plowshares for the black Illinois loam. The forge, the kiln and the mill consolidated the conquest of the wilderness.

When the American soldiers, with rifles, shovels and an ox, arrived August 17, 1803, they found four cabins in the vicinity of the "Chikago River." One of these had been built by Chicago's first settler, Jean Baptiste Point Sable, a half-breed negro; another was lived in by Ouilmette, half-caste Pottawattomie chief; a third by a mysterious Pettle, of whom there is scant record; and the fourth, vacant, was owned by the Indian trader, John Kinzie, and had been built by Point Sable. These were all log houses, built

American fashión, but of the most primitive type. Let us dismiss them with this briefest of mention and consider Chicago's first architectural monument, old Fort Dearborn. The first Fort Dearborn undoubtedly belongs to the large category of buildings where the historical interest transcends the architectural. In this case one can hardly see the architecture for the history; so the historical growths will be cleared away as much as possible to expose to view the rude but not unbeautiful fortress.

The chronological sequence of the principal events leading to its establishment is as follows: The successful outcome (for the Americans) of the Revolutionary War and the brilliant exploits of George Rogers Clark secured Illinois for the United States, as set forth in the Treaty of Paris in 1783. The Indians of the Northwest, continuously stirred up by the British, who had no confidence in the stability of the young republic, were not reconciled to their new masters, notwithstanding numerous treaties. In consequence, St. Clair, the new United States military governor at Cincinnati, in 1791 met the most disastrous defeat the white man had ever suffered at the hand of the redskin. It was not until the decisive victory of General Wayne (Mad Anthony) over the Indians at Fallen Timbers that the Americans secured a lasting grip on their new-won empire. In the Treaty of Greenville with the Indians in 1795 General Wayne inserted a clause that secured a piece [6] of land six miles square at the mouth of the Chicago River suitable for the building of a fort. Such a fort became vitally necessary when the United States by the Louisiana Purchase acquired another empire, this time from France. So in 1803

---

[6] This, the birth certificate of Chicago, is worth repeating again: "One piece of Land Six miles square at the mouth of the Chikago River emptying into the Southwest end of Lake Michigan, where a fort formerly stood."

General Dearborn, Secretary of War, ordered the site to be investigated and the fort to be built forthwith.

It is fair to assume—in fact, we can be certain—that the "supplies" shipped by Captain Whistler on the good ship Tracy contained all necessary tools and some building material, such as nails and hardware, and we can also be sure that both young Lieutenant Swearingen's courageous band marching through the wilderness from Detroit and Captain Whistler's schooner contained skilled mechanics, such as pit-sawyers, masons, wheelwrights, and armorers. Apparently the government expected the soldiers to wrest from their environment all the material except the iron.

Lieutenant Swearingen arrived at the mouth of the river August 17, 1803. In his diary he noted that the stream was ninety feet wide and about twenty deep, but that it was practically stagnant, owing to a sand-bar across its mouth at the lake shore, forcing it to turn south some half mile before it could find entrance to the lake in greatly reduced volume and current owing to its seepage through the sand.[7] Where the river meets the impasse and turns south there is a low bluff about twelve feet high at the elbow. Doubtless the young lieutenant had his eye on this strategic point, though he returned to Detroit before the building operations were commenced.

About the same time the Tracy arrived bearing the family and goods of the new commandant, Captain John Whistler, a middle-aged man. The fort was soon laid out on the elbow of sandy bluff and the work begun. We should like to know if the experienced captain had any plan wherewith to build a fort. We have the famous Whistler plan from which the replica of Fort Dearborn at the Century of Progress was built, but as this shows

[7] This is a common phenomenon in rivers flowing into Lake Michigan. A similar situation exists today in the Dead River south of Zion City.

a considerable number of incidental buildings and dwellings outside the compound it was obviously made after the fort was completed. It is therefore a record—not a building plan.[8] The government had, however, been building forts for protection against the Indians for years and undoubtedly had developed a standard specification. For instance, the fort must be commodious enough to hold not only the garrison but the neighboring settlers. There must be a double stockade with certain minimum heights. There must be one or more blockhouses on the corners commanding the approaches and enfilading the space between the stockades. The blockhouses must be built with a projecting second story with holes in the floors and loopholes in the walls. The corners must be closely trimmed so no foothold might be offered the redskin. There must be barracks and officers' quarters and a magazine. There must be a main entrance with heavy gates and possibly a concealed postern gate. There must be a well and a flag-pole. Necessary buildings for stores, trading, etc., might be within or without the stockade.

We may assume therefore that Captain Whistler, armed with these general instructions, his own experience and the skill of his carpenters, laid out the fort to accommodate his force and to fit the site selected. Instead of four blockhouses,[9] one at each corner, he used but two, one at the northwest corner of the stockade and the other at

[8] There are other evidences. No dimensions are given for the buildings nor are their interior arrangements shown. The plan is not in the technique of an architect, nor even of an engineer, but the drawing of the trees and the façades of the buildings indicates the artist's point of view.

[9] There were many stockaded forts in Illinois roughly contemporary with Fort Dearborn. The most complete was Camp Russell near Edwardsville, built in 1812 and armed with Louis XIV cannons brought from Fort Chartres, Fort Armstrong on Rock Island, Fort Clark (Peoria), 1813. The old French forts of the seventeenth century—Crèvecoeur, St. Louis, Massac—were of the stockade type. In fact, Fort Chartres was the only one of masonry. Many small Blackhawk forts existed, for instance, the one at Apple River near Galena. See *Historic Illinois* by Randall Parrish.

the southeast corner. As the north and east sides were protected against Indian attack by the river and the lake one wonders a little at this disposition. The southwest corner was the vulnerable spot and this was left exposed except for the enfilading fire from the blockhouses one hundred and twenty feet away. In the second fort this vulnerable point was the only one honored with a blockhouse.

With the exception of the Whistler sketch there is no known contemporary representation of the first fort, although there are many pictorial restorations, some of them old enough to have been made from descriptions of those who had seen it. These show porches, most of them two-story, on five of the buildings, the officers' and soldiers' barracks, the hospital and even the contractor's store. The Whistler plan does not show these porches nor were they included in the restoration at the Century of Progress.

For eight or nine years life was rather dull at the fort. In accordance with the governmental policy of keeping the garrison busy the soldiers were doubtless instructed to build these verandas during this period. It is significant that the veranda became popular—one might almost say was invented—at this time. After the Revolutionary War, when good houses began to be built throughout the South, verandas became necessary and beautiful features of all of them. Perhaps the earliest and most typical were at Charleston, South Carolina. What testimony to the fortitude of fashion that it should brave the Indians and the wilderness to appear at the farthest-flung outpost of American civilization!

More interesting than a description of the various buildings of the first fort, which can be seen from the drawings, would be an attempt to determine exactly where it stood in relation to the present city. The main entrance gate, about the middle of the south side of the stockade, was where the middle line of Wacker Drive intersects the middle line of Michigan Boulevard. The bronze tablet on the face of the London Guarantee Building memorializes the position of the second fort, which extended west and south of the first.[10]

The second fort in some respects is a more fascinating subject for research than the first. Destroyed in piecemeal, its last vestige survived until 1871, so that we have some photographic evidence of its appearance, and at the Chicago Historical Society some of the actual logs[11] of the blockhouse.

In the Historical Society's Library is a manuscript narrative of one Moses Morgan who died in 1877. He was a carpenter recruited at Buffalo for the construction of the second fort, and his recollections of an event occurring some sixty years before are illuminating and interesting. "In the early part of 1816," he said, "an architect arrived at Detroit who was sent by the War Department to have full control and to superintend the construction of the new Fort Dearborn according to plans and specifications furnished him by the government at Washington and not subject to any change at the request of any officer or commander whatever." One might infer from this that the Whistlers, father and son, may have taken liberties with the plans and specifications, if any, furnished them by the government for the first fort, which might account for the fact that the southwest corner, its most vulnerable point, was left unfortified except for its palisade. He then went on to tell that the architect, who seems to be name-

---

[10] H. A. Musham, *Report on the Location of the First Fort Dearborn.*

[11] Other timbers are built into the ceiling of the cloister of the First Presbyterian Church, Chicago.

less, enlisted six or seven mechanics in Buffalo, some of whom turned back at their first sight of Indians, and one gay fellow who decamped with an Indian squaw. This must have sorely depleted the original band of craftsmen, but, undaunted, the architect addressed them, urging greater efforts on their part and pointing out that this was no ordinary "chinked log cabin" sort of job but that "all logs must be squared." The first job of the soldiers on landing was to plant vegetables for winter use while the busy architect with the aid of Ouilmette, which he spells "Wilmette," and another "half breed," Robinson, selected trees for felling. These were rolled into the lake and rafted to the sand-bar at the mouth of the river. In the meantime, a schooner arrived from Detroit with sawn lumber to erect emergency shelters for the stores in a temporary camp on the lake shore, a quarter mile south of the fort.

One wonders if Pine Grove Avenue be not the where-abouts of the choice "growth of large pine four miles north of the river," pointed out by Ouilmette. This description, if correct, would locate this stand of pine, the trees of which were so large that they had to be sawn into planks on the spot. No vestige of this pine remains. The only sections of the lake shore in the city which retain their original character are two short stretches in Rogers Park at Touhy Avenue still covered with scrub oak. These supertrees, Mr. Morgan goes on to say, were especially reserved for building the roof and flooring for the officers' barracks.

The second Fort Dearborn has never excited the historians of Chicago, so their descriptions of its building and even of its site lack vividness and precision. It was not "built on the same spot," one says,[12] but, considering

[12] Blanchard, *The Northwest and Chicago.*

the center of the parade as its center, it was moved several feet to the west. In other words, Michigan avenue would extend straight through the parade ground, and the blockhouse would be buried under the west side of the London Guarantee Building.

This second fort had only one blockhouse and only one palisade, though it had bastions on the corners. The magazine and one of the store buildings were of brick, both probably built later. Most pictures of the second fort show the very substantial lighthouse immediately to the west. The Hon. John Wentworth, at the ceremonies connected with the unveiling of the tablet in 1881 on the site of the blockhouse, tells us that the second fort was occupied in June, 1816,[13] and that it continued to be garrisoned until 1823. In 1828 it was reoccupied. The garrison was finally withdrawn in 1836, a few years after the Black Hawk War scare, and the fort gradually sank into unromantic decay. The officers' quarters were moved to the corner of State and Thirty-third Streets, and the barracks and other buildings within the palisade were first used for other purposes and then destroyed. The palisade made excellent firewood, and the blockhouse was removed in 1857.[14] The last vestige of the fort disappeared in the fire of 1871. A reproduction of a photograph,[15]

[13] John Wentworth, *Fort Dearborn,* "Fergus Historical Series," Vol. 16.

[14] Gales, *Early Chicago and Vicinity.*

[15] Pictures of the second Fort Dearborn, Chicago Historical Society:
Old wood-cut "Fort Dearborn as rebuilt 1816."
Photograph of an engraving dated in pencil, 1820.
Woodcut "Chicago in 1830 from the lake" (apparently a copy of engraving above with the addition of a few Indians).
"Second Fort Dearborn looking south from the river"—no date.
Photograph of rude engraving much the same as the 1820 picture except that houses of Dean, Wolcott, Beaubien and Kinzie are labelled.
Plan-Map G-17 by Lieut.-Col. J. B. Graham, 1855.
Photograph described above, taken in 1858, shows barracks, lighthouse, but no blockhouse.
Lithograph, "Fort Dearborn, Chicago in 1820," published 1867.

dated in pencil 1858, apparently from the mast of a ship, does not show the blockhouse, but does show both the officers' and soldiers' barracks. As a final word on the second fort, all of the illustrations have two-story porches, a feature of the first fort that seems to have justified its continued existence for its comfort and good looks. As the sole conscious gesture in the direction of beauty these porches rank as the earliest examples of architectural design in the history of Chicago.

The present fashion among architectural historians and critics is to attempt to ignore the reality of architectural style. To these enfranchised souls Architecture is one beautiful expanding bloom or just one big happy family. However, it is certain in the history of European civilization that approximately every five hundred years there has been a basic change in architecture. This applies to construction and ornament together. We are seeing the beginning of one of these five-hundred-year-epoch cycles at the present time. It is also certain that every thirty years or so there is a change in the stylistic ornamentation of buildings. Both of these phenomena, the basic and the superficial, are discussed in terms of "style."

The basic are founded deep in the necessities and aspirations of the human soul, which seem to burst the bonds of precedent at these five hundred year climacterics and leap forth on a new path. The superficial belong to the phenomena of fashion and have to do almost solely with adornment. These variations, always local or national, that come a generation or so apart are conveniently called "styles."

Thus we find our city at its birth, 1803, in the architectural epoch which we call the Renaissance and at the tag end of the architectural style which we call Colonial. As our American Colonial style ran a long and vigorous course of some one hundred seventy-five years it is entirely sensible that natural variations in such a length of time should have special names for their definition. These are, with their approximate dates: Early American, 1630-1720; Georgian Colonial, 1720-1790; Post-Colonial, 1790-1820—each one properly designated as a style. If they can be described in a sentence it would be safe to say that the Early American is quasi-mediaeval in appearance, based on memories of Elizabethan and Jacobean architecture in England; that the Georgian was inspired by work done under Queen Anne and the first three Georges; and that the Post-Colonial, or Federal, was inspired by French architecture from the time of Louis XVI to Napoleon. It must be understood that all of them not only underwent a sea change but, translated into American materials by American craftsmen unhampered with any exact knowledge of the subject, emerged as national expressions, if not creations, well worthy of their position in the roster of styles.

While the man with the rifle and the axe is oblivious of style, not so his successor with the plow and the plane. A house of boards must have a doorway. For reasons probably of pride and prowess man from the beginning of time has ornamented his doorway. From the lion's skin nailed over the dubious entrance to the Chaldean's hut of mud to the chromium and black enamel of a portal on Astor Street the urge has been always the same. Hence style, like seeds in the beak of a bird or, if you prefer, like pollen on the thigh of a bee, is carried wherever man can penetrate, and rests for a while.

Immigration to the Illinois country in the latter years of the Revolutionary War lagged behind the white stream that percolated through the forests south of the Ohio. This was owing to the hostility of the Indians fostered by our kinsmen the British, reluctant to give up a royal domain even after it no longer belonged to them. The entering wedge seems to have been the settlement of Marietta, Ohio. After this the rich and invigorating land of Michigan and Illinois was to be had for the taking. Sticking to latitude, as the human migrant always does, we find Northern Illinois settled by New Englanders. We also find it is a decade or two behind Kentucky, Tennessee, Southern Indiana and Southern Illinois, largely settled by Virginians and men from the Old South. This is reflected not only in its more vigorous growth but in its styles of architecture.

At the time of the settlement of the more southern areas the last phase of the Colonial, the Post-Colonial, sometimes called the Federal, style was in vogue. In the South it flourished particularly. Jefferson, the father of the style, had established its norm at Monticello and at the University of Virginia. Charleston is full of examples, and the White House in Washington spread its fame. It was the most sophisticated of the Colonial styles, one which was impossible to achieve without numerous delvings into the handbooks. In fact, it really required the erudition of the architect. Whatever the two-story verandas of Fort Dearborn were like in detail, in point of time and in spirit they were of this Post-Colonial family. The serious settlement of Chicago and Northern Illinois did not begin before 1830, and by that time the Post-Colonial style was decidedly "old hat."

The twenties in Chicago were days of germination, of pre-natal stirrings. The lusty young wild onion had not more than heaved the soil. Certainly the social life of Chicago in the somnolent twenties could hardly be called stirring. Its high spot was the Winnebago scare in 1827. Although terror-stricken settlers poured into Galena and

Chicago, the Indian rebellion was put down by a one-man army consisting of Governor Lewis Cass of Michigan, who travelled 1600 miles in a birch-bark canoe through the Indians' country, bluffing the chiefs into peace treaties and completing the great circle at Chicago. It is regretfully recorded that we gave the brave general a sorry welcome, for he spent a whole night at our front door, stuck in the mud of the Chicago portage.

Henry R. Schoolcraft visited Chicago in 1820 and made a sketch of Fort Dearborn and the surrounding houses. He predicted a rosy future, but could list not more than sixty inhabitants beyond the military, and a dozen cabins. Far different the vision of Major Long in his government survey. He found the "climate inhospitable, the soil sterile, the scenery monotonous." The village, he said, consisted of a few huts of log or bark—"low, filthy, disgusting, displaying not the least trace of comfort and inhabited by a miserable race of men." Otherwise we assume the Major found Chicago delightful.

Far more pleasing than the Major were two other characters that dominated the infancy of the city. Gurdon Hubbard captures our hearts when as a boy of sixteen, approaching Chicago after the long trip along the eastern shore of the lake, he could restrain his impatience no longer and climbed a tree like a moccasined Zacchaeus, beholding afar off the whitewashed walls of Fort Dearborn like silver in the sunlight. A history of architecture grants no permission to an author to write of the lives of others than architects. Cannot I say, at least, that he was truly nature's nobleman? In him the primitive virtues and physical prowess of the pioneer were united to the sophistication and polish of the gentleman. Besides he had the vision of a prophet, and of all the woodsmen he alone knew when and how to lay down the rifle for the

pen, and the beaver skin for the ledger. Gurdon Hubbard
lived to the age of eighty-five and died in Chicago in 1886.
He remains a symbol both of the old Northwest and of the
building of Chicago—a hero with the wilderness on one
hand and the city on the other.

Our other famous citizen of the twenties was John Kinzie. The name Kinzie, hardly second to Dearborn, was
our best known surname for many decades in the growing city. He is in a vague way known as the Father of
Chicago. M. M. Quaife, the eminent historian of the old
Northwest, thinks that Captain Whistler instead is entitled to that honor and argues that John Kinzie was
press-agented into pre-eminence by his brilliant daughter-
in-law, who, in her fascinating narrative of *Wau-Bun*,
wielded a pen dipped in the romance of the old Northwest
and in the glory of the Kinzie family, with a generous
admixture of her own vivid imagination. Mr. Quaife's
argument seems to me based on certain of Kinzie's tem-
peramental frailties, such as his violent temper, which
led to homicide on one occasion, and his involved marital
experiences rather than on any lack of accomplishment.
As in the case of the more appealing figure of Gurdon
Hubbard, this is no page on which to eulogize John Kinzie
or even to recount his deeds. Technically speaking, we
should only record his rebuilding of a house antedating
Fort Dearborn and his appeal to the Secretary of War
that the fort should be rebuilt after its destruction.

John Kinzie, as adventurous explorer, silversmith, and
fur-trader, occupied a log cabin on the north bank of the
river in 1804, a bit to the east of the present Michigan
Boulevard bridgehead. This cabin was built by the
mulatto Point Sable and during the construction of the
first fort was occupied by the ladies of the garrison. Kinzie
moved here with his family in 1804, in ample time for the

massacre. In this tragedy he gave sage but futile advice to the commandant and marched forth with the others to what must have appeared to him as certain destruction when he could have remained behind in security.

Four years after the destruction of the fort he returned to Chicago, apparently enlarging his house to its well known appearance with its continuous porch across the front, its gable ends, its picket fence, the four poplar trees in front and the huge cottonwood behind. With no record or accurate drawings, it appears to be a log house enlarged, covered with siding and whitewashed. At any rate, through the early days, it was the manor house of Chicago's first family, the welcoming fireside to the youthful Hubbard.

The author of *Wau-Bun,* Mrs. John H. Kinzie, lists the buildings of Chicago as of 1831. Since she refers to them as established edifices, it is fair to assume that they were built in the previous decade. She writes that there was at the southwest corner of North Water and Wolcott, now State Street, the Agency House called "Cobweb Castle" because of its long tenure by a bachelor. (Dr. Alexander Wolcott, the Indian Agent, lived here from 1820 to 1830.) "A substantial compact little building of logs hewed and squared, with a center and two wings." Around about was a "collection of log buildings, the residences of different persons in the employ of the government." She mentions "the blacksmith, striker and laborers." There must have been as well the house of Antoine Ouilmette, after whom Wilmette, Illinois, is named, which stood a little west of the Kinzie house. He was the only white resident left in Chicago after the massacre of 1812.

There was one more house on the north side of the river near the forks, built by a "former resident of the name of Miller." This "former resident of the name of

Miller" was no less than Mrs. Kinzie's brother-in-law—
to rattle a few bones in the Kinzie closet. Across the river
from this domicile was a new house (Sauganash Hotel)
built by Mark Beaubien. "It was a pretentious two-story
building with bright blue wooden shutters—the admiration of all." The only houses on the West Side in the
twenties were, apparently: "a small tavern kept by Mr.
Wentworth"; and nearby two or three log cabins, evidently
of the humble sort, as they were occupied by reformed
Pottawatomies such as Chief Robinson and Billy Caldwell, the Sauganash. "A little remote from these" was a
square log building, designed for a schoolhouse and used as
a church on the occasional visits of an itinerant preacher.

Close at the heels of Dearborn and Kinzie in its famili-
arity to Chicagoans is the name of Clybourne. Just what
the contribution of the Clybournes was to the cultural or
civic life of the little town I do not know. But the geog-
rapher and the architect are grateful to the family. The
Clybournes were pioneers even in this outpost village, for
they pushed far out on the North Branch, and named
their place "New Virginia." The original log house was
replaced early in the '30's with a mansion flaunting a
two-story porch, perhaps the first house with real architectural pretence in Chicago.

At the other extent of the map, four miles up the South
Branch near what is now Racine Avenue, was Lee's farm
called "Hardscrabble," a pioneer term for hard scratching
or poor pickings. At Lee's place occurred the premonitory
murder by some skulking Indians that presaged the massacre at Fort Dearborn.

There were other cabins not important enough to
chronicle, and there was, to end the list, the most pretentious of all, at least in size, the factory building. The policy
of the government of going into the business of selling

goods and buying furs direct with the Indians was a bone of contention for many years in Congress. The purpose of the enterprise was truly altruistic. Even with the red light of burning cabins against the sky and the whoop of the redskin in the air the Indian had many champions who tried to see that he got a square deal.

The first quarter of the 18th century was the golden age of the fur trade, and the great log "factory" was a busy and highly interesting place. The temptation to draw a picture of the Chicago "factory" is hard to resist: the puncheon floor piled high with beaver pelts; the rude shelves packed with those products of civilization already regarded as necessities by the Indian; the alert young American factors—Belknap and Varnum—and the silent red men, each with one eye on a shining new rifle and the other on the scales and his mind filled with Heaven knows what thoughts. The trading-house system was abolished in 1822 and the trading-house relegated to the humdrum purposes of a general store.

All the historians agree that in Chicago days were quiet in the twenties, "as dull," as one author says, "as the thirties were lively." Nevertheless, through the long hectic perspective of one hundred ten years they seem far from unattractive. The fort and the very few log houses listed prove that Chicago was a very primitive pioneer outpost still in the heart of an almost undefiled wilderness. As the winters were the same then as now it is not difficult to visualize the prairie and even the fort under a mantle of snow. In the spring the prairie west of the river and the low land between its south branch and the lake became flooded, and a unanimous shout from every commentator attests that the resultant mud was the deepest, the blackest and the stickiest that the world had ever seen. In fact, the mud of Chicago runs like a theme song or a *leit motif* through every account down to the sixties. Perhaps the richest anecdote is one told of young Long John Wentworth, who, observing a stranger buried up to his armpits in the mud of State Street, offered to be of assistance. "No thankee, Sir," the man replied, "I've got a good horse under me."

But in the summer the mud had dried and the great prairie, beginning at the west border of the river, became a gorgeous carpet of waving grass and wild flowers. "Green and flowery" was the youthful impression of one native daughter.[16] In autumn came the wild life, and if ever the expression "a hunter's paradise," which stirs the blood and awakens the longing of every man, could be applied in the fullness of truth to any land that fabled spot was Chicago. From the edge of the forest on the north bank deer watched with startled eyes the doings of the usurper. Those magnificent birds, the prairie chickens, now so nearly extinct, were then so plentiful in the prairie west of the river that they sold for five cents apiece; and the sloughs on the prairie, the great marshes at Calumet and Tolleston and the river itself were filled with ducks, geese and swans.

John Kinzie, by day a stern trader and man of affairs, at night took out his fiddle and set the moccasined feet of the traders and the leather boots of the young officers a-jigging. Mark Beaubien, father, not *at* but *of,* twenty-two, was the genial, careless and popular Boniface of the first tavern. His better-known older brother, Jean Baptiste, an old Indian trader and squaw-man, lived south of the fort. His residence on the Fort Dearborn reservation established the famous Beaubien Land Claim, which had Chicago realtors and lawyers by the ears for a generation or more. There were Billy Caldwell, half-breed chief of

[16] Mrs. Joseph E. Ward in *Chicago Yesterdays* by Kirkland.

the Chicago Pottawatomies, and Ouilmette, the French squaw-man, who in the twenties must have been venerated as the oldest inhabitant as he had been on hand to welcome Captain Whistler in 1803. There were the army officers Helm, Hamilton and their subalterns; and, off and on, the tall and broad-shouldered figure of the youthful trader, Gurdon Hubbard, filled the doorway of his welcoming hosts. Perhaps the most fascinating visitor, because of his mystery, was the roving son of Alexander Hamilton. Of such was the little coterie who wiled away the peaceful decade of the twenties.

CHAPTER II

Childhood · 1830-1855

IF the twenties were somnolent and almost mediaeval, not so the lively thirties. The first year of the new decade saw the beginning of Chicago's brilliant metamorphosis from a primitive outpost to a village, and before seven years had flown she was in name at least a city. In fact there was no town of Chicago before 1830. Until that time the name "Chicago" designated a region that stretched as far away as the Desplaines river. That first year, 1830, saw Chicago platted and surveyed. In 1831 Chicago was designated the county seat of Cook County, the first post-office was established at the Forks of the river, a lighthouse was built just west of the fort, the first sawmill and sash and blind factory were established, and the first frame building, the Sauganash Hotel, was erected. In 1832 the first bridge across the river, a floating log bridge, was constructed—rather surprisingly over the South Branch near Randolph Street. The year 1833 saw the improvement of the harbor commenced, the town incorporated, the *Chicago Democrat* first published, the Tremont House erected, as well as three "First" churches—Catholic, Presbyterian and Baptist.

Of the many accounts of early Chicago none paints a more vivid picture than that of Charles J. Latrobe, who

27

visited the village in 1833 at the time the government was negotiating for the purchase of the Indian lands of the Pottawatomies and for their removal across the Mississippi River.

"I have been," he writes, "in many odd assemblages of my species, but in few, if any, of so singular a character as that within the midst of which we spent a week in Chicago. This little mushroom town is situated upon the verge of a perfectly level tract of country, for the greater part consisting of open prairie lands, at a point where a small river whose sources interlock in the wet season with those of the Illinois, enters Lake Michigan. It however forms no harbour and vessels must anchor in the open lake, which spreads to the horizon to the north and east, in a sheet of unbroken extent.

"The river, after approaching nearly at right angles, to within a few hundred yards of the lake, makes a short turn, and runs to the southward parallel to the beach. Fort Dearborn and the light-house are placed at the angle thus formed. The former is a small stockaded enclosure with block-houses, and is garrisoned by two companies of infantry. It had been nearly abandoned till the late Indian war on the frontier made its occupation necessary. The upstart village lies chiefly on the right bank of the river above the fort. . . . .

"We found the village on our arrival crowded to excess; and we procured with great difficulty a small apartment, comfortless and noisy, but quite as good as we could have hoped for. The Pottawatomies were encamped on all sides,—on the wide level prairie beyond the scattered village, beneath the shelter of the low woods which chequered them on the side of the small river, or to the leeward of the sand hills near the beach of the lake. . . . . Meanwhile the village and its inhabitants presented a motley scene. The fort contained within its palisades by far the most enlightened residents, in the little knot of officers attached to the slender garrison. . . . . Next in rank to the Officers and Commissioners, may be noticed certain store-keepers and merchants resident here; looking to the influx of new settlers establishing themselves in the neighborhood, or those passing yet farther to the westward. . . . . Add to these a doctor or two, two or three lawyers, a land agent, and five or six hotel-keepers. These may be considered as stationary, and proprietors of the half a hundred clapboard houses around you. Then for the birds of passage, exclusive of the Pottawatomies of whom more anon—emigrants and land-speculators as numerous as the sand. You will find horse-dealers and horse-stealers,— rogues of every description, white, black, brown, and red —half-breeds, quarter-breeds, and men of no breed at all;—dealers in pigs, poultry and potatoes;—men pursuing Indian claims . . . . and claims for pigs that the wolves had eaten; . . . . Indian agents and Indian traders of every description, and Contractors to supply the Pottawatomies with food. The little village was in an uproar from morning to night, and from night to morning. . . . . All was bustle and tumult, especially at the hour set apart for the distribution of rations. . . . . The interior of the village was one chaos of mud, rubbish, and confusion. Frame and clapboard houses were springing up daily under the active axes and hammers of the speculators, and piles of lumber announced the preparation for yet other edifices of an equally light character. . . . . I loved to stroll at sun-set out across the river, and gaze upon the level horizon, stretching to the north-west over the surface of the Prairie, dotted with innumerable objects far and near. . . . . Far and wide the grassy prairie teemed with figures; warriors mounted or on foot, squaws and horses.

Here, a race between three or four Indian ponies each carrying a double rider, whooping and yelling like fiends. There a solitary horseman with a long spear, turbaned like an Arab scouring along at full speed; groups of hobbled horses; Indian dogs and children, or a grave conclave of grey chiefs seated on the grass; . . . . and there a party breaking up their encampment, and falling with their little train of loaded ponies, and wolfish dogs, into the deep black narrow trail running to the north."

Eighteen-thirty-four started off merrily with Chicago's first divorce suit and murder trial and the arrival of the first piano, and ended with the start of the great immigration from the East and the beginning of Chicago's first real estate boom. Modest at first, the boom was fanned into flame the following May with the opening of the government land office in Chicago and the sale of public lands. Beginning with the sale of the school section between State and Halsted and Madison and Twelfth for $38,865, and culminating in such fantastic prices as $60,000 in 1836 for a parcel on Lake Street that had been bought for $300 two years earlier,[1] the boom ended with Chicago's first panic and depression at the end of 1837.

In the meantime the almost forgotten Pottawatomies held their last powwow, so eloquently described by Judge Caton. Fort Dearborn passed into limbo with the final evacuation of its troops in December, 1836; the first railroad (to Galena) was chartered; and the first house built from an architect's drawings, after which it is almost an anti-climax to remark that on March 4, 1837, Chicago was incorporated as a city. With a "never say die" spirit in the first year of the depression we brought forth our first fire-engine and our first home-made steamboat, and

[1] Lewis and Smith, *Chicago: The History of Its Reputation.*

finally ended the decade with our first great fire and our first brewery.

All these and other events in the economic and social history of Chicago have affected in varying degree the course of its architectural history, yet where the course is merely augmented and not changed in direction or significance they cannot properly find a place in this story. There was, for instance, the nation-wide-heralded Illinois-Michigan Canal. This almost fabulous waterway, first envisioned by Joliet in 1673 and begun on July 4th, 1836, paralleled the old Chicago portage and was supposed to supplant it, but by the time of its dedication, 1848, the beaver and the trader had both long since disappeared and multiplying steel rails pointed to the imminent obsolescence of the canal. Nevertheless, the sale of the "canal lots" started the "boom" and made Chicago in the mid-thirties the cynosure of a nation. In like degree but in reverse direction the banking panic of '37 collapsed the value of Chicago's real estate and well nigh ruined her reputation, but neither affected in any vital way her architectural destiny.

Whether we accept or reject Chicago's claim to blood relationship with the Colonial style on the slender evidence of Fort Dearborn's verandas, the fact remains that her real architecture began with the Greek Revival.

This Greek Revival style, which we hear more and more of as its survivors steadily decrease and the appreciation of its beauty and interest as steadily increases, is one of the most fascinating of all our native fashions.

The Historic American Buildings Survey has done a splendid work in Illinois in photographing, measuring and collecting data on our early architecture. This survey shows that the Greek Revival was *par excellence* the style of the later and permanent settler. The devotion of the horny-handed, axe-wielding, plow-pushing pioneer to this exotic, erudite and difficult architectural fashion is one of the most eloquent phenomena in the little-studied realm of the influence of fashion on civilization. It was well called in its own time "the Greek mania." As everyone knows, the Classic dream had been the theme song in English literature and art throughout the eighteenth century, but as far as architecture is concerned knowledge of Greece was certainly of the stuff that dreams are made of. The story runs something like this:

Two young Englishmen, James Stuart and Nicholas Revett, not content with the essence of Greek architecture, determined to examine the substance. Accordingly in 1752 they went to Athens and made careful drawings of those godlike temples whose noble brows crown the Acropolis. These were published in magnificent tomes by the Dilettante Society of London and became a necessary part of every gentleman's library, for in those days Architecture was not only one of the politest of accomplishments but one of the most popular. In the days of the Regency in England the Greek Revival reached the height of fashion. It spread to Germany and to France, where it appeared in a modified form called *Néo-Grec,* and to America where, astonishing to relate, it achieved its greatest popularity and its widest distribution. State house, church, mansion and cottage donned with equal celerity and with almost equal grace the tunic snatched from the shoulders of Athena, and the acanthus bloomed in a wilderness that hitherto had known only the Indian corn and the wild onion.

Benjamin Latrobe, one of the ardent young Whigs who adored George Washington as the symbol of Liberty, came to America in 1796. As engineer and architect in the office of Cockerell the elder, an English architect, he had learned the nuances of the new style at its fountain-head. He practically brought it to the New World in his grip-sack and used it in building the important Bank of Pennsylvania, 1799-1801. By this building he kindled an architectural conflagration that swept like a prairie fire to the Gulf of Mexico and as far west as the Great Salt Lake. The fuel that fed the flame and without which it would have gone out in its first spark was a curious little device known as the "builders' handbook." The master craftsmen, such as MacIntyre, who fashioned in colonial days those lovely doorways that embroider the streets of Salem, had gone to their reward—and let us hope it was glorious—while the professional architects who had created the preceding Post-Colonial were rare birds and, besides, a bit beyond the adventuring age. A vast building program faced a lusty young nation devoid of architects, and the humble little handbook slipped into the breach, and into the breeches pockets of the builders, and saved the day! In the Burnham Library of the Art Institute there is an almost complete collection of these powerful little books. They date all the way from 1798 to 1861.

The earliest and most prolific author of these handbooks was Asher Benjamin. He wrote *The Country Builders Assistant,* 1798, *The Practical House Carpenter,* 1830, and *Elements of Architecture,* 1843. The first, which you will observe is written in Post-Colonial times, is illustrated with the Roman Classic orders, but the others are almost exclusively Greek! These books contained the "Orders"—Doric, Ionic and Corinthian—very carefully drawn (taken, of course from Stuart and Revett's *Antiquities of Athens*) with minute directions for their translation into wood, plaster and stone. The little books also showed how to build stairs, cut rafters, even fashion domes.[2] Every carpenter who followed in the train of the covered wagon had one in his kit. Hence, the nation-wide distribution of the Greek Revival.

Undoubtedly the dream of the pioneer builder or the carpenter-architect, if you please, was a building with a portico, whether it be courthouse, church or dwelling, and a portico after the fashion of a Greek temple with columns and a pediment. This could usually be managed with the public buildings, but was out of the question in the house unless it ascended into the upper brackets of the "mansion." He was also beset with a major difficulty with regard to his material. He well knew that his idols were built of marble, but they might as well have been built of gold. The only stone available in Northern Illinois was the outcropping of the Niagara formation found along the lower Desplaines. This was difficult to carve and its rough texture seemed a rude substitute for the silken skin of a Greek marble wall. Brick was a necessity for the walls of the larger buildings, but for the smaller it must be confined to the chimneys and foundations. However they found ready to their hands an inexhaustible quarry of the finest building material in the world— American white pine. Across Lake Michigan, only a day

[2] Handbooks in use between 1795 and 1860.
1798—*Country Builders Assistant* by Asher Benjamin.
1800—*Ibid.*
1806-11-16-20-26-27—*American Builders Companion* by Asher Benjamin.
1820—*Rudiments of Architecture* by Asher Benjamin.
1829—*Young Builders General Instructor* by Minard Lefèvre.
1830—*Practical House Carpenter* by Asher Benjamin.
1835—*Beauties of Modern Architecture* by Minard Lefèvre.
1839—*Practice of Architecture* by Asher Benjamin.
1843—*Elements of Architecture* by Asher Benjamin.
1843—*Rural Architecture* by Edward Shaw.
1845—*American House Carpenter* by R. S. Hatfield.
1851—*Architecture of Country Houses* by A. J. Downing.
1851—*The Architect or Practical House Carpenter* by Asher Benjamin.
1852—*Rural Architecture* by L. F. Allen.
1860—*Carpenters New Guide* by Peter Nicholson.

or two away by schooner, stood the primeval forest— millions upon millions of growing columns as straight and as pure as those Pentelic shafts of their imagination. The forest died in giving birth to the city, and clear white pine today is as precious as mahogany. It now costs about $80 a thousand board feet, equal to a thousand square feet of boards one inch thick, but it was laid down in the late thirties in Chicago at $20 per thousand; and so Chicago became a white pine city.

The method of construction is important. In the East through colonial days wooden houses had been "framed." The method was as follows: First, a heavy squared timber called a sill was laid on top of the foundation wall. At the four corners and on the sides of windows and doors heavy upright posts, the height of the first story, were erected on this sill and braced between other uprights called studs or scantlings, which were placed between. These supported in their turn, at the second story level, a continuous timber horizontal called a "girt," and the whole was thoroughly braced with diagonal timbers. The same process was duplicated for the second story and the framework crowned with a continuous timber called a plate, on which rested the ends of the rafters forming the sloping roof. The ends of the floor-beams rested in slots cut into the sides of the girt in a manner known as mortising. In fact, all of the framing in a similar way was mortised, tenoned and spiked or pegged together. All the lumber was adzed or sawn by hand. All this, doubtless, made a strong house, but it was a tedious, expensive and wasteful method of construction; yet it followed the settler with sturdy steps into a new land. Coincident with Chicago's lusty infancy, steam had supplanted the water-wheel and the ox in operating the saw-mills. The circular steam-driven saw made it economical to saw lumber in much smaller units. "Two by fours," "two by twelves," "one by tens," etc., of pine supplanted the ungainly chestnut and oak hand-hewn logs and clumsy boards painfully sawn by the pit sawyers. Our carpenters in the middle thirties not only had these fragrant argosies, schooner borne, dumped at their feet, but they were faced with a sudden and unexpected influx of settlers and a fantastic real estate and building boom.

We now come to one of those architectural inventions, born of the fertility of Chicago, that has made her throughout her history the most generous of the cities in her gifts to Architecture, and that is balloon construction.

In this form of construction the carpenter took these slender 2 x 4 and 2 x 6 studs, set them on end the entire height of the wall, and placed them about sixteen inches apart on centers and jointed their tops together with another 2 x 4 laid horizontally. Instead of "mortising," that is, fitting the heavy floor-beams into huge girts, he laid the ends of these joists, two inches in thickness, on a slender "ribbon"—a 1 x 6 board let into the sides of the studs. Holes for windows and doors were cut out wherever desired, and 2 x 4 rafters were set about 20″ on center, their ends resting on the plate. After the "frame" was completed, the builder had a light wooden cage which he proceeded to enclose with a covering of boards called "sheathing." This clever idea is called "balloon construction." Although it is extremely light it can be made extremely strong. It depends for its strength really on the thoroughness of the nailing.

In fact it was often called "spiked construction" as distinguished from girt buildings, which were sometimes known as "pegged" construction. The following advertisement from the first issue of the first newspaper printed in Chicago, November 26, 1833, is significant and eloquent of the birth of an epochal discovery: "Cut nails from 3 p. to 20 p. of superior quality for sale by the keg or less quantity of John Wright."

Many a "balloon construction" house, like a gigantic tumble-weed, has rolled along the prairie under the urging of a tornado without serious injury to the house at least. At any rate and without the aid of tornadoes "balloon construction" spread over the entire continent and is still cock of the walk in so far as the small house is concerned. Its supremacy is about to be challenged by the "pre-fabricated house." The conflict will furnish a good show for the next generation.

John Root paid his tribute to balloon construction. "This early type of dwelling has made the growth of the West possible," he said. "Unlike the early dwellings of wood erected in the East no expert carpenter was needed, no mortise nor tenon nor other mysteries of carpentry interfered with the swiftness of its growth. A keg of nails, some two by four inch studs, a few cedar posts for foundations and a lot of clapboards, with two strong arms to wield the hammer and saw—these only were needed and these were always to be had." [3]

Who invented balloon construction? For most certainly invented it was. I have already pointed out the necessity of rapid building in the booming thirties and of the opportunity at hand in the gleaming piles of sawn white pine. Our principal authority is Charles Cleaver. This early settler, English by birth, came to Chicago in 1833. His establishment at the foot of Thirty-eighth gave the name Cleaverville to the entire neighborhood. By trade he was a tallow renderer. Energized by Chicago's lively climate, he branched into civic and building ventures and

---

[3] *House Design in Middle West,* 1889.

left some interesting and valuable reminiscences.[4] He says that previous to 1833 most of the houses were of logs, "just as they came from the woods," and even the more pretentious "were built of hewn logs." The North Branch had been dammed five or six miles up the stream where a small sawmill was located and run by water-power. There was, as well, a small steam saw-mill south of Division Street, also on the North Branch. Both of these mills sawed only the trees that grew in the neighborhood—oak, elm, poplar, white ash. This lumber was used green and much trouble was encountered, he says, in the subsequent warping and splitting. This poor stuff, of which he found only about 6000 board feet on hand, sold for $60 a thousand. Shipments of lumber, still quoting him, greatly increased the supply during the summer of 1834. He thinks most of it came from Canada, but even in 1837 timber was still scarce.

This date, 1837, is the year he ascribes, at least inferentially, to the invention of "balloon framing," for he writes, "Heavy timber for frame buildings soon after came into disuse, as it was found the present way of putting up frame buildings was much stronger and better."

G. W. Snow, an old settler, has the credit of originating the idea. William Bross, better known as Deacon Bross, Chicago's first "booster," also bears witness.[5] After describing with some detail the "balloon fashion" he continues, "This cheap, but for a new town excellent mode of building, it is claimed, was first introduced or, if you please, invented in Chicago and I believe the claim to be true." Last and most authoritative of all are the words of Chicago's first architect, J. M. Van Osdel, who arrived

[4] *Reminiscences of Chicago during the Forties and Fifties,* "The Lakeside Classics."

[5] William Bross, "What I Remember of Early Chicago," *Chicago Tribune,* 1876. Reprinted in *Reminiscences* by Lakeside Press.

in 1837. In the second of a series of papers which he wrote for the *Inland Architect* in 1882 [6] he says, "Mr. Snow was the inventor of the 'balloon frame' method of constructing wooden buildings which in this city completely superseded the old style of framing with posts, girts, beams, and braces. The great rapidity in construction and the large saving in cost, compared with the old-fashioned frame, brought the 'balloon frame' into general use."

So much for balloon construction. Lest it be considered but a minor contribution to the science of building, let it be remembered that all frame houses and most frame buildings of various sorts, whether faced with siding, shingles or stucco, throughout the breadth of the land and for the last seventy-five years have been built of balloon construction.

Balloon framing was about as far distant as it is possible to conceive from any type of construction that the ancient Greeks ever employed, yet so adaptable was it that it was always the type used, say after 1840, except for masonry buildings, for houses in the Greek Revival style.

Our excursion down a by-path of construction has been more extended than perhaps contemplated; let us therefore return to our architecture. As has been said, the complete dream of a temple form with a portico, pediments and a finished entablature was seldom realized. So the average house was boiled down to one with narrow pilasters on the corners instead of the portico, a low gable instead of a pediment, and a cornice instead of an entablature. An orthodox entablature, the crowning feature of a wall, consisted of three horizontal elements— the architrave below, the cornice on top, and the frieze

[6] *Inland Architect and Builder,* No. 1, Vol. 1.

between. Further economy was effected by omitting even
the cornice across the end walls under the gables, returning it only a matter of a foot or so. This small piece of
cornice on each side of the front and back of a building
is the surest indication of the Greek Revival style before
it completely disappeared about 1855 or 1860 with the
coming of the "Parvenu" fashions of the Civil War period.

An equally eloquent symptom is the profile of the
mouldings. Roman mouldings, according to the school-
books, are combinations of the arcs of circles. The theory
is that the enormous building projects of the Roman Empire were carried out by vast crews of slaves, who had to
have simple methods for what they did. Greek mouldings,
however, were subtle affairs, done freehand with an artistic touch or, if with an instrument, they took the erudite
forms of conic sections. All of this was set forth with great
care in the handbooks.

In those days there were no factories for the making
of moulded trim, doors, stairs, etc. These features were
manufactured by expert carpenters on the job or in the
shop, and the mouldings were cut or "run" with planes
carrying sharp blades shaped to the proper profile. These
Greek shapes are very characteristic and are instantly
recognizable when you get to know them. On the old
pioneer houses they occur in the cornices around the door
and window openings and on the interior trim.

There were other characteristics. The stair balustrades
were very simple with plain tapering spindles and simple
turned newel. Fireplaces again struck the simple note—
one-inch slabs of slate or marble or wood and the plainest
of shelves. The walls and ceilings were of plaster, whitewashed or painted. When it came to the plan the limitations of the carpenter-architect were dragged into the
light. He might copy his architectural features very ac-

ceptably from his handbooks, but there was no such open sesame in the planning of the building. Hence most of the Greek Revival houses and larger buildings, too, showed cramped hallways and an uninteresting succession of rooms, planned with little regard to their special uses and often poorly lighted.

Returning to the open air again with some relief, we sympathize with him in his roofing troubles. The Greek temple model requires a roof with a very low or flat slant. If such a roof is of shingles, which were at first his only available roofing material, it is sure to leak, and the snow lies heavy upon it. Again the heavy cornice and low-ceiling heights for the smaller houses often forced him to use very short windows for the second story—charming and characteristic from without, but almighty inconvenient from within unless you liked to get down on your knees for a breath of fresh air or for a look at the great outdoors. The pleasant two-story porch seems to have died in Chicago with Fort Dearborn, and, as the Caryatid porch of the Erectheon was too much even for the handbooks, the pioneers went mostly porchless except for a flat uncovered stoop. In "mansions" such as the William B. Ogden, the Clybourne and the Widow Clark houses, some of these inconveniences were obviated. Here ceiling heights ran to the other extreme, and there were porches and verandas galore.

In 1854 Booster Bross boasted that Chicago had one hundred fifty-nine miles of sidewalks and twenty-seven miles of planked streets. Lining these sidewalks and streets were thousands of houses, churches and commercial buildings. By an act of the Legislature in February, 1853, the city limits were extended to Thirty-first Street on the south, and Fullerton Avenue on the north, and the western limit was Western Avenue, a city six miles long and in its

widest part four miles. The Chicago Fire in 1871[7] ac-
counted for all the buildings east of the north and south
branches of the river and from the north limits of the
city to Congress Street. There was also an irregular area
on the west side, stretching east in fan shape from Mrs.
O'Leary's cow-barn. Therefore there was an area five miles
long and over two miles wide west of the river and another two miles long and over a mile wide south of Congress that were not touched by the Fire. Here there are
over twelve square miles built up more or less thickly in
1853, and the puzzle is, after making big allowances for rebuilding, where all these buildings are today. We are interested in them at this point because they were, presumably,
all in the Greek Revival style, which was, with an occasional Roman exception, the only style the carpenter-
architects had. Milwaukee, Waukegan, Rockford, Galena,
Springfield are still all salted with little Greek buildings,
but in Chicago, with so many more, the Greek savor almost utterly disappeared. A little later on we will spread
the pitiful list on the record.

The architecture that had continued its course through
exaltation and depression in gradually increasing *tempo*
resulted in a city that must have presented, say, in 1853
a singularly uniform and harmonious appearance. This
does not mean that young Chicago bore the slightest
resemblance to ancient Athens or that any large number
of its buildings gloried in porticos or even columns. Still,
the Greek parentage united every building into one big
family by its facial characteristics. Furthermore, all com-

[7] A. T. Andreas in his *History of Chicago,* 1884, attributes the great extent of the
conflagration of 1871 to the prevalence of wood buildings of balloon construction.
He says the only buildings which were saved were a few that had been moved from
the town to its outskirts. Among them was a block of buildings on Lake Street,
moved to State near Twelfth. This building had a "corniced pediment of Grecian
Ionic order." "In 1839 this was the finest business block in the city."

mercial or business structures were of pretty much a uniform height, five stories, the limit that human legs would carry a tenant without protest.

A singular uniformity prevailed in the color scheme—white or cream for the walls, be they wood or stone, and green for the shutters and trimmings. The houses, most with gabled ends and porches, sat a comfortable distance back from the street with a lap of green lawn. Edging the lawn or "front yard" was a fence of white palings or of cast iron filigree and beyond the wooden sidewalk a row of shade trees. Here and there above the green trees and the white gables pointed the white fingers of the churches, and, dominating what seemed to be an almost somnolent community, rose the stately classic cupola of the Court House. It is really sad that this youthful and beautiful city, through act of God and of man, has utterly disappeared save for the names and locations of its streets. Today the lake, in those days a friendly next-door neighbor, we push farther and farther from us, as though we disliked it.

Of this charming white and green city, bathing its feet in the blue of Lake Michigan, only a small number of buildings are standing today that could possibly have been built in or about 1853. Among these are the Second Baptist Church, 1856 ("First" when built on the southeast corner of La Salle and Washington, now the Aiken Institute), which stands on Morgan and West Monroe Streets, bereft of its steeple, and the Widow Clark house, which once stood at or about Sixteenth and Michigan Avenue and which was moved to 4526 Wabash Avenue, where it still remains. There are also: a very interesting row of houses, frame with pedimented windows, at 616 Ada Street; a tumble-down store at Grand Avenue, west of Halsted, said to have been built before 1850, but

later rebuilt beyond recognition; a row of frame buildings reported to have been Civil War barracks, built
about 1860, and only faintly reminiscent of the Greek
Revival; and a house at 163 Halsted having a cornice
return on its façade. With the exception of the Aiken
Institute and the Widow Clark's house, these few are,
at best, doubtful and feeble specimens. At 517, or there-
abouts, on Morgan, set far back from the street, there
is an interesting house with heavily corniced windows
and a Classic door. In the seventies it was obviously
raised and a brick ground-story of "Eastlake" ancestry
built beneath it. The house next to it is old, too, dating
apparently, from the sixties.

As a miserable climax to Chicago's feeble collection of
Greek Revival buildings may be mentioned an unnum-
bered frame structure on Milwaukee Avenue near Grand.
The skin of the building looks of the vintage of the
eighties, but in the little pediment is the date 1850, the
earliest I have been able to find. The date was either
removed from an earlier building on the site or, very possibly, the older building lies within its later skin.

This unbelievable poverty in the architecture of the
older day in Chicago can be somewhat relieved even today
by trips through the country-side, for one with the seeing
eye and understanding heart will still discover homes of
pioneers, usually back from the road-side and refuged in
the trees. Such finds make any excursion a delight, a compensation even for gasoline fumes, speed fiends and road-
side advertising.

In referring to the old Court House I used the name of
Van Osdel for the first time. This famous (to architects)
man is always spoken of as Chicago's first architect, and
no man has a better right to the appellation. Perhaps it
is the vision we have of him, handed down through several

HENRY B. (WIDOW) CLARK FARMHOUSE

As originally built during the 1840's near Sixteenth Street and Michigan Avenue

HENRY B. (WIDOW) CLARK HOUSE TODAY AT 4526 WABASH AVENUE

A unique reminder of early Chicago

generations of blue prints and draughting-boards, that makes his memory flash upon our inward eye—his tall figure and patrician mien, his gentle manner, his unbending principles causing him to call himself a "Garrisonian Abolitionist," and, above all, the blue tailed coat with brass buttons which he always wore. I cannot go into his early life except to say that his name was John M. Van Osdel and that he was born in Baltimore July 31, 1811.[8] His life, as far as we are concerned, began in New York in the fall of 1836, when he met the Hon. William B. Ogden. It so happened that Mr. Ogden was not only Chicago's most prosperous and energetic citizen, but he was also looking for an architect to build a mansion in the little mud-swamped village on the lake. He was impressed by Van Osdel, who was only twenty-five, and offered him the job. Van Osdel evidently started at once to work, for we find him not only making the long trek with his plans under his arm in the spring of '37, but bringing as well "the glazed sash and the stair rails, trimmings and carvings," and doubtless many other items— but we must postpone a little the description of this famous house. He returned, but only for a year or two, to New York in 1840, where he was associate editor of the *American Mechanic,* now known as the *Scientific American.*

Van Osdel wrote in his reminiscences, published with the first number of the *Inland Architect* in 1882, that when he came to Chicago in 1837 there were not one thousand buildings in the city, and of these less than twenty were of brick and more than half one-story cottages. The roofs, he said, were without exception shingled, for tar and gravel roofing was unknown. This would seem to indicate that all roofs were sloping or pedimented, as

[8] Thomas E. Tallmadge, *Dictionary of American Biography,* article on Van Osdel.

you can't cover a flat roof with shingles and stay dry. He said there were no architects and little demand for them. In fact, he abandoned the profession himself for a little while, and built two steamboats—the first constructed in our city. He asked us to believe, and we must for his probity has never been questioned, that in 1844 the building contractors of the city came to him with the proposition that if he would establish an architectural office they would agree to build no more without plans—the architect's perfect dream. He opened his office on Clark Street between the City Hall and the Post-Office, and in that year erected a block of four-story brick houses on the north side of Lake street between Clark and Dearborn. Van Osdel stated that these were the first ever built in Chicago according to plans and specifications, excepting, I suppose, the Ogden house, and that his fee was one hundred dollars. A sole architect in Chicago in the forties must have been a busy man. In 1844 six hundred buildings went up—he surely couldn't have done them all, but he tells us that in three years he earned $32,000, and certainly most of the principal buildings were to his credit. During the Chicago Fire with his usual resourcefulness he dug a huge pit and therein saved his plans. After he dug them out, like so many roasted potatoes, he proceeded to put up in eighteen months over eight thousand lineal feet of frontage (one mile and three fifths!), in which there were some buildings of great size. This very likely explains the disastrous similarity of the buildings erected directly after the fire to those which were destroyed. Many of them were reproduced from these and other old plans.

Van Osdel lived until 1892, having seen in succession the Post-Colonial, the Greek Revival, the Parvenu and the Romanesque Revival sweep across the stage. We as-

From Alexander Hesler's Panorama in Chicago Historical Society Collection

CHICAGO 1858 VIEW FROM TOP OF COURT HOUSE DOME

Looking northeast, the Sherman House is in left foreground, with the two-storied Saloon Building appearing above on the southeast corner of Clark and Lake. On the lake rim at the right are the twin Sturges and Buckingham grain elevators, one of which still survives. Box-like structures such as the five-storied Potter Palmer store, slightly above and to the right of the Saloon Building engulf the delightful earlier town, represented by the Greek Revival buildings on the east side of Clark Street.

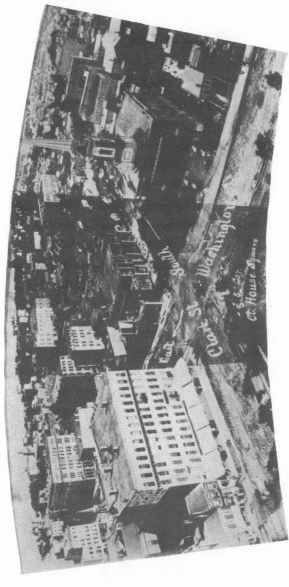

From Alexander Hesler's Panorama in Chicago Historical Society Collection

CHICAGO 1858 VIEW FROM TOP OF COURT HOUSE DOME

Looking southeast, the First Methodist Church is under construction at the center. Almost directly above on the lake rim is Terrace Row with St. Mary's Catholic Church on Wabash and Madison and Bishop's Palace farther to the left. The Unitarian Church steeple appears behind the Bryant and Stratton building. The First Presbyterian structure, already vacated, is on the southwest corner of Washington and Clark. In right center to the left of its spire can be seen the Post-Office, as yet roofless. To the right is Old Trinity Church.

sociate him, however, with the Greek Revival and the Parvenu periods. His was a splendid example of pioneer energy and shrewd common sense, rising above such things as technical or aesthetic training.

Van Osdel was a true son of the builders' handbook— in fact, he wrote one himself, "The Carpenters' Hand Book"—and his father had been a high class builder before him. Nevertheless we architects wonder how a man without technical training could have built such a structure as the second Court House in 1853, or the great Palmer House after the Fire, mentioning these merely as samples of his work. As his creations almost span the whole life-history of Chicago nearly to the World's Fair, it seems better to list his buildings, ever changing in style, as they appear in our story.

Let us now go back to 1837, the year that Chicago's first architect arrived in the infant city, and review the buildings that his careful and appraising eye observed. This date is an excellent one for an inventory, because it is not only about a hundred years ago, but because Van Osdel, at his date of writing in 1882 states that no building then existed which had been built prior to 1838. You will remember his assertion that there were not over a thousand buildings of all degree, of which less than twenty were of brick, and more than half frame cottages. He lists, possibly in their order of architectural importance, first, the brick ones on the north side: the Lake House, 1835, on the southeast corner of Rush and Michigan (Austin Avenue). This big building is usually depicted in views of the second Fort Dearborn. It was three stories high, "elegantly furnished throughout and cost nearly $100,000." Public-spirited citizens like Gurdon S. Hubbard, John Kinzie, Dr. Egan, and others, financed it. In 1837, we are informed, it had a French chef and a printed menu! Its fortunes gradually declined, however, until the Great Fire ended its troubles; its location must have been bad. St. James' Episcopal Church, 1837, a "pretentious semi-Gothic building with a square brick tower" on Cass (Wabash) between Michigan and Illinois. John Kinzie gave the lot and Gurdon Hubbard and Dr. Egan were vestrymen. The especial pride of the congregation was a huge mahogany pulpit, eighteen feet wide and fifteen feet high. A two-story house on Indiana Street (Grand Avenue) near Dearborn and two stores on North Water near Cass (Wabash) all belonging to William Norton, who is said to have built the first bridge across the river at Dearborn Street.

On the west side he mentions a house on Jackson and Canal owned by La Framboise, an Indian chief, and the famous mansion of Archibald Clybourne, built in 1836 on Elston Avenue just south of Cortland Street. This building in its days of glory would have been an imposing pile in any location. Its two-story columned and pilastered portico, its windows and doors with their carved colonial lintels, its gables and coupled chimneys would have seemed more at home on the banks of the James than on a muddy prairie of the old Northwest. When the streets finally reached out to this architectural pioneer, they found that the builder had been a sorry prophet, for the back door now faced the thoroughfare and the noble portico frowned on the rear yard.

In the "South Division," in the brick building class, was the Court House on the northeast corner of the Public Square (Clark and Randolph). Van Osdel describes it as being about sixty by thirty feet, with court room and jury rooms on the main floor, and the clerk, recorder and vaults in the basement. The front was ennobled with a four-columned, free-standing portico of wood in the Greek

Doric order, which made it automatically a true son of the Greek Revival. Across the street (where now stands the Sherman House) was the City Hotel.[9] This considerable building was eighty by one hundred feet and three stories high. It was built and owned by F. C. Sherman. It housed the City Council and was the progenitor of a race of Sherman Houses, all occupying this site. After one or two unimportant structures, Van Osdel describes the "Saloon Building," "saloon" meaning in this instance a huge room. It stood on the southwest corner of Lake and Clark and was about eighty feet square and four stories high. Any account of it states with glee that the chimneys were forgotten and had to be added later where wanted. The Saloon Building was, in fact, the Faneuil Hall of the infant city. One of its rooms served as the City Hall from 1837 to 1843. Here in 1837 the youthful Stephen A. Douglas captured Chicago Democracy, and here a year later an enthusiastic booster was almost laughed down by predicting that children already had been born who would live to see the city with 50,000 inhabitants. The building, from an old cut, appears to be a typically plain affair with a simple Classic cornice and plain stone lintels over the windows. The three-story building of the State Bank of Illinois at the southwest corner of South Water and La Salle, the Charles Chapman house on Wells and Randolph, and the two-story house of P. F. W. Peck, on the southwest corner of La Salle and Washington, completed the list of brick buildings in the spring of 1837. Van Osdel doesn't list the frame houses, but of them the mansion of William B. Ogden doubtless soon reigned supreme. There must also have been Billy Caldwell's house, built in 1828 by a grateful government for the half-breed's efforts to

[9] Andreas (*History of Chicago*) says a later City Hotel was on the corner of State and Lake and was built in 1848.

preserve peace between the whites and redskins. It stood on State and Chicago Avenue in 1828.

There is a regrettable lack of documents, especially pictures, of the houses of the fifties. Since many of these houses persisted until the Chicago Fire, one would think there would be excellent photographs unless they were burned up along with the buildings. The most distinguished house in Chicago at this time was that of William B. Ogden, standing in the center of the block bounded by Cass (Wabash) and Rush, Ontario and Erie. Mr. Joseph T. Ryerson, who came to Chicago in 1842, writes in his memoirs that "the house was a large double two-storied conspicuous house with portico and columns, and broad steps. There were stables, out-houses, and green-houses." He also says that the house was built by a land company and purchased by Mr. Ogden in the panic of 1837-38. But as we know all about Van Osdel's making the plans and building the house, Mr. Ryerson was obviously in error. Mrs. William Blair in her reminiscences observes: [10] "There is not today in our wealthy and luxurious city, there never has been in fact, a residence more attractive, more homelike, more beautiful than that of Mr. Ogden." She writes of the fine growth of various trees and adds: "In the center stood his 'double' house built of wood; a broad piazza extended across the south front. A large conservatory and fruit houses added to its beauty and comfort." A "double" house today usually means a two-family house, but as Ogden was a bachelor and properly entitled to only half a house, we have to go back to find that in the fifties a double house was one with a hall in the center. Mary Drummond writes that "the rooms were spacious and delightful. The dining-room with its windows opening in three sides, being one of the most

[10] Kirkland, *Chicago Yesterdays.*

beautiful rooms in Chicago." An inspection of the "Bird's-Eye View of 1853" through a strong glass certainly shows a house of large size and great dignity. A pedimented portico extended to the south and a large gabled wing to the east with the typical returned entablature of the Greek Revival style. A high cupola surmounted the center, and the whole place was a fitting lodge for Chicago's first citizen.

Although almost entirely without pictures or descriptions, even a bare list of some of these old houses of the fifties is redolent of the spirit of old Chicago. Their exact locations are known. There was the house of Justin Butterfield, two-story frame with a "double front" and a large garden on Rush Street near Michigan (Austin Avenue), and the two-story brick house of John H. Kinzie on the corner of Cass (Wabash) and Michigan. The latter was the son of old John and the husband of the author of *Wau-Bun*. Their home was the social center of the Episcopalians. Isaac N. Arnold's "long low frame house" occupied a corner of Dearborn and Ontario. Arnold's name bobs up in almost every page of Chicago's early history, from the time he landed in the infant city in 1836 until his death, as lawyer, congressman, writer and public-spirited citizen. McCagg, whose house stood at Clark and Chestnut, was a great name, at least socially, related to the Ogdens, the Sheldons, and the Butlers. A son wrote: "I remember our house with much clearness, the two parlors, dining room and library as well as my mother's bed room and the nursery all on the ground floor in the good old generous way." [11] Joseph Ryerson describes in considerable detail the house he built for his maiden sister, Anne Ryerson, on Ontario Street in 1850.[12] This house, he says, was the first three-story brick dwelling

[11] *Ibid.*　　　　　　[12] *Ibid.*

built in Chicago. It cost $5,000, had a 25-foot front and was about 50 feet deep. The kitchen and dining-room were evidently on the entrance floor, as he speaks of a "good cellar under all." He says that it was a "Philadelphia Style" house and that the plans had been drawn in Philadelphia. The "Philadelphia Style" in the fifties was noted for its simplicity—a completely unadorned red brick front without horizontal bands or even a cornice. The windows were bordered by plain white stone or marble lintels and stone or marble sills. The entrance door, which Mr. Ryerson proudly describes as "the first double front door and vestibule" in Chicago, was designed in restrained Doric style, had a square transom light, sometimes side lights, and was painted white. In fact, with the exception of a few great porticoed houses like the William B. Ogden house and the churches, the houses in Chicago of the Greek Revival period were extremely plain. This was partly on account of limited facilities for manufacturing elaborate building material, but mostly because of the habit and necessity for economy.

Perhaps this assurance of the plainness of the exteriors of these Greek Revival buildings turns us more willingly to enter their front doors. The ordinary house, not the "double house," had the entrance hall and long stairway at one side, and the parlor and sitting-room on the other, opening into each other with folding-doors. The end of the hall normally opened into the dining-room, and that into the kitchen. In 1853 grades had not yet been raised, so the houses were without benefit of basement, for, because of a lack of sewers, prevalence of ground water made them impossible. Such a house on Rush and Ohio, on the site of the old Virginia Hotel, was moved into by Mrs. Leander McCormick in December, 1838. She writes her sister in Virginia in an enthusiastic and excited strain "we are happily fixed and are much pleased with our new home and friends." This house, of which she made a rough sketch which we would like very much to see, apparently was of this typical arrangement except that the sitting-room served as a parlor, for she says, "beautiful flowered red and green carpets in the chamber and parlor, and when the folding doors are open, the stove in the chamber will heat both rooms." She adds, "There are three rooms upstairs, one finely furnished for Cyrus." She speaks of a dozen beautiful mahogany chairs, a "beautiful bureau" and a "twenty-four dollar card table."

It might be interesting right now to find out what facilities there were in the Chicago of the late thirties for making beautiful bureaus and twenty-four-dollar card tables. It is only necessary to turn to the June 8 edition of the *Chicago American,* 1835, to read that "J. Rockwell continues to manufacture cabinet furniture at the stand on South Water Street where he keeps constantly for sale, a complete assortment of Cabinet Furniture, consisting of sideboards, secretaries, bureaus, commodes, wardrobes, lockers, dressing, card, pier, center and common tables, ottomans, divans, crickets, and foot stools. Also a variety of chairs and bedsteads which with other articles in his line will be made after the latest New York and Paris fashions."

Let us now take a farewell view of the city as of 1853-55. All, all are gone, the old familiar faces, and to reconstruct Chicago in its early guise, we must perforce turn first to the lithographs and wood-cuts, and later to the primitive photography of pre-Fire days. No better picture of Chicago in its adolescence can be found than the imaginary Bird's-Eye View from Lake Michigan made in 1853. This is a crayon drawing, evidently the work of an archi-

CHICA

From a reproduction of a crayon drawing originally published by Smith Brothers & Co., New York, found in Andreas, "History of Chicago," Vol. I

1853.

tectural draughtsman. It represents Chicago in its last condition of architectural purity just before it became seduced by the florid pretensions of the Victorian and Continental styles.

Ascending to the imaginary elevation of the "artist of the crayon view" we see a delightful rural city spread out before us. The general character of its architecture, the Greek Revival, has been described, perhaps too much, and its salient natural features were then as they are now—the blue lake unchanging and unchangeable at our feet, the silver T of the river dividing the city as now into three parts. Two bridges cross the main river at Wells and Clark, two, the north branch at Kinzie (one a railway bridge) and three cross the south branch at Lake, Randolph, Van Buren. All are swing bridges of one kind or another. We see in addition a number of ferries. At the mouth of the river there are two short projecting piers, one with a lighthouse. Parallel with the shore, protected by a breakwater, runs the Illinois Central Railway on piles. Between it and the shore stretches a lagoon and west of it an informal greensward bounded by fences and trees. Michigan Avenue except at its lower end seems to be little more than a lane.

Although the city limits in 1853 extended from Fullerton to Thirty-first Street and from the lake to Western, the buildings of any consequence were confined between Chicago Avenue and Congress Street and not more than a block or two west of the river. Nevertheless the youthful city seems cast in heroic mould. The wide streets, the noble squares, the most simple and direct of city plans prophetically lies open and ready for a mighty development. It is easy to determine from this accurate and beautiful drawing the centers of the various activities of Chicago in 1853. Along the river on both sides are the warehouses, wholesale houses, factories and elevators. Both sides of Lake Street and north to South Water are given over to shops, hotels and office buildings. Randolph has business houses, hotels, a few residences and the public square with the classic Court House. South of Washington the city rapidly becomes residential and ecclesiastical, with fine houses up and down Wabash Avenue and on La Salle Street, interspersed with the churches. South of Madison the houses are scattered and small. Except along Wabash and the lake front there are few trees in what is now the downtown district, while on the north side they are abundant. This is easily explained by the fact that Chicago grew too fast to alter the natural situation, which was treeless south and west of the river and forested north.

The north side, north of Kinzie and east of Dearborn, is given over to residences and churches, most of them not remarkable in either size or elegance, but yet often in the center of large lots and surrounded by trees and picket fences. The lake shore, as usual, is neglected, and buildings east of Pine Street (Michigan Avenue) are for the most part miserable affairs. The building which dominates in no slight degree the entire scene is the Court House, just erected by Van Osdel, which we have described.

Next are the churches. For the design of the highest and most splendid of these, the Roman Catholic Cathedral of the Holy Name, the artist had to anticipate a bit, for the Cathedral was not dedicated until Christmas Day of 1854. The size was surprising for a church in an outlying parish—eighty-four by one hundred and ninety feet, eighty-seven feet to the ridge pole, with a spire two hundred and forty-five feet high. The architects were Burling and Baumann. *The Chronicle* states that the Cathedral was built of Milwaukee brick and in the Gothic style and that it had stained glass windows depicting Biblical scenes and was to cost $75,000 to $100,000. It was of course entirely destroyed in the Chicago Fire. It stood on the site of the present Cathedral in the block bounded by Chicago Avenue, Superior, State and Cass (Wabash) streets.

Just as interesting and more grateful to the eye was St. Mary's Roman Catholic Church, constructed after various vicissitudes on the southwest corner of Madison and Wabash. Erected in 1833, it was a true child of the Greek Revival, of brick with a portico fifty-five feet wide and supported by four Ionic columns. The first St. Mary's had been built of lumber on the southwest corner of State and Lake in May, 1853. August D. Taylor is variously spoken of as its architect and carpenter. There were at least five other Catholic churches, but none of architectural importance.

A church that looms up in the picture with great prominence, partly on account of its unobstructed site, is the Second Presbyterian, which stood on the northeast corner of Wabash and Washington. This is the second "Second"; the original church of frame stood on Randolph near Dearborn. Contemporaries described it as "the most imposing and inviting church edifice in Chicago," and one enthusiast at the cornerstone-laying in 1849 predicted it would still be standing a thousand years hence. Twenty-two years later the blazing city saw it go up like Elijah's chariot of fire. The building was seventy-three by one hundred thirty feet, with walls fifty feet high. Andreas is authority for saying it would seat eighteen hundred people. Its strong congregation, led by Robert W. Patterson, was proud of its size and power for good and also of the stained glass windows and the huge clock. The architect, John Van Osdel, was doubtless proud too of its Gothic architecture, about which no one in those days

From Alexander Hesler's Panorama in Chicago Historical Society Collection

CHICAGO 1858 VIEW FROM TOP OF COURT HOUSE DOME

The First Baptist Church of 1853, later removed to the west side and known as Aiken Institute, appears prominently on the Chamber of Commerce site. Across LaSalle Street is the P. F. W. Peck home accompanied by other Greek Revival brick residences of prominent citizens. "Hoyne's Folly," four-storied wonder of the forties, is in the right foreground already outscaled by many larger commercial structures.

CHICAGO 1858 VIEW FROM TOP OF COURT HOUSE DOME

Looking southwest, Metropolitan Hall occupies the center and the Briggs House is in the same block, next corner west. The four-storied arched Scammon's bank is on the extreme right northeast corner of LaSalle and Lake. Adjoining Sharp's Corner in the left foreground is a group of hastily built frame cottages, probably of balloon type, which were so typical of early Chicago.

could gainsay him. The curiously spotted stone of this old church can be seen today in the Presbyterian Church of Lake Forest, whither some of it was moved after the Fire. This stone may also be seen in the Second Presbyterian Church, Twentieth Street and Michigan Avenue.

Farther west on Washington Street four other churches raised their white steeples. Beyond these on the southeast corner of La Salle and Washington can be seen the First Baptist Church in process of building. There was a noble lineage of Baptist churches in early Chicago, beginning with the Temple Building erected in 1833 on the southwest corner of Franklin and South Water. If we except a log house at the Point used for religious as well as living purposes, this was the second church built in the city. St. Mary's Catholic Church had been erected at State and Lake earlier in 1833. This Temple Building, parenthetically, was a true community building shared alike by the Methodists and Presbyterians and serving the purpose of a school-house as well. Dr. Freeman, pastor of the first Baptist, met his death from exposure, having spent two December nights and a day on the wide prairie watching over his sick horse, stricken during a pastoral visit. On this same site a noble edifice was erected in 1844. It was obviously a creature of the builders' handbook. A Greek hexastyle (six-columned) portico with Ionic columns held a pediment fifty-five feet wide, which in turn supported a belfry of Sir Christopher Wren lineage and a spire one hundred twelve feet above the sidewalk. It seems unbelievable that this building, brick at that, cost only $4,500.[13] This church was destroyed by fire in 1852 and was succeeded immediately by a greater one, which stands unique today, having been moved before

[13] Andreas, *History of Chicago.*

the Fire to Morgan and West Monroe, as our sole sur-
viving monumental building in the Greek Revival style.

Another Baptist church in the temple form, though
this time with Greek Doric pilasters, was built in 1843 on
the west side of La Salle between Washington and Randolph. This was called the Tabernacle Baptist Church.
It was founded on a schism brought about by the insistence of certain Baptists on praying for the slaves as the
"oppressed."

Close to the First Baptist Church, in fact on the next
corner, Clark and Washington, stood the First Presbyterian. What a temptation to sketch the history of the
Presbyterian Church, to speak of Jeremiah Porter, who
preached in the carpentry shop of Fort Dearborn, May 19,
1833, and who wrote, "The first dreadful spectacle that
met my eyes on going to church was a group of Indians
sitting on the ground playing cards, and as many trifling
white men standing around to witness the game!" The
Presbyterians dedicated their first church in January,
1834, at the southwest corner of Lake and Clark, but in
due course built in 1848 the brick church on Washington
street. This also was of the prevailing classic mode, with
a colonial steeple, and it cost $28,000. So rapidly did the
congregation increase that the property was sold in 1855
and the church pulled down for the purpose of building
three new churches, one in each division of the city.

The Methodists also were unable to resist the lure of
Washington Street, so we find them in 1838 picking up
their church—a "frame building, twenty-six by thirty-
eight feet, twelve foot posts, sheeted and shingled roof;
a neat pulpit, a platform for table and chairs"—and mov-
ing it across the river from the North Side and setting it
down on the northeast corner of Washington and Clark
streets. Enlarged from time to time, it was succeeded in

1845 by a brick building, sixty-six by ninety-five feet, which cost $12,000. It had a stone basement eight feet high and walls thirty feet high, and the apex of the spire was one hundred forty-eight feet from the ground. In architecture it was Greekish, with Doric pilasters, a temple roof and a steeple very, very similar, clocks and all, to that of the Baptists. This church, too, had its anti-slavery problem, as on the occasion when one William "Box" Brown, a fugitive slave who acquired his middle name through his technique of escape, delivered from the pulpit an anti-slavery address, causing the pro-slavery communicants to "buzz around like enraged bumble-bees."

The Universalists seemed to be particularly architec-turally-minded. Although their church on Washington just east of the Methodists was not a grandiose affair, it was unusually interesting in design, employing Ionic columns "in antis" (facing each other in a recess). The steeple, more properly a cupola, was a well-designed com-position with a little dome instead of a spire. Less than ten years later increasing numbers emboldened them to build "a monument of architectural grandeur and beauty" on the southwest corner of Wabash and Van Buren. The church had a real architect, W. W. Boyington.

The North Side needs no apologies, for it as well had no lack of churches. Dominating them in height and bulk was the Gothic Cathedral of the Holy Name at Superior and State, which has already been described, and over nearer the river was the famous St. James' Episcopal, famous on several counts. In the first place its site on the corner of Cass (Wabash) and Illinois was donated by John H. Kinzie and in consequence the church had a nar-row escape from being known as "the Kinzie Church." It was built in 1837 and, you will remember, it was listed by

Van Osdel as one of the "less than twenty" brick structures in the city in that year. It was certainly the first
brick church. The entire cost of this building including
"organ, bell, carpet and lamps" was $15,500. However,
events, including churches, moved rapidly in the fifties,
and we find St. James' in 1857 in a great stone structure on
Cass and Huron, its present location. This building cost
$60,000 exclusive of the tower. We read of no pro-slavery
difficulties in St. James', but there was a church trial in
which one of the counts was that the rector, the defend-
ant, was wont to slip a shot-gun under his seat in his Sab-
batical excursions and to come back with his buggy full of
prairie chickens. He probably made the mistake of neglect-
ing to distribute them among his vestrymen. Only one
other church, I promise you—the North Presbyterian.
Here again there was a rapid succession of buildings—first
a "small frame structure with a pepper box steeple," built
in 1848, to be succeeded in 1852 by a larger building on the
southwest corner of Illinois and State (Wolcott Street in
those days), to be shortly followed by a structure, big for
any time, seating eleven hundred people with a tower one
hundred ninety-four feet high. This building at the corner
of Indiana and Cass (Wabash) had in its basement lec-
ture rooms, a Sunday school, etc. We are told its architectural style was Romanesque. Just before the Fire this
church united with Westminster and became the Fourth
Presbyterian Church, whose beautiful Gothic architecture in its latest building arrests many a footstep and lifts
many an eye on Michigan Avenue today.

It will not be necessary to describe in any detail the
commercial buildings. They were exceedingly plain. The
windows logically were holes in the walls, lining up, of
course, vertically and horizontally but without intermediate cornices or architectural embellishment. The earliest

had plain stone lintels, which became moulded later on, often with cast iron trimmings. The same is true of the lowest story. Plain brick piers separated the window spaces at first, to be supplanted later by cast iron ornamental columns and large sheets of glass. The cornices in the old times were extremely simple, but by 1853 jigsawed wooden brackets began to appear. If you wish to see how Chicago business buildings looked in the fifties go to St. Louis along the old river front. There they are still standing.

The Court House, then as now, rises from the civic block bounded by LaSalle and Clark, Randolph and Washington streets. It was also, then as now, occupied jointly by city and county. This handsome building was in the Greek style, notwithstanding an arch or two here and there. It was of the Doric order with low pediments and a full entablature resting on Doric pilasters. The four wings were roofed with flat domes and in the center rose a high cupola. The building was completed in 1853 and cost $110,000. The walls were faced with gray marble taken from the Lockport, New York, quarries.[14] John M. Van Osdel was the architect and superintendent. In Hesler's photograph you can glimpse some of the neighboring buildings.

A later and more authentic record is the photographic panorama made by Alexander Hesler in 1858 from the Court House cupola. At that time, the city had just begun to show the influx of those new fashions—the Victorian Gothic and the French mansard. As a small boy, I boarded with my family in Mr. Hesler's home in Evanston. I remember, of course, the old gentleman distinctly—his black skull-cap and his blacker eyes, his snow white beard and energetic movements, his love of flowers and his

[14] *Ibid.*

willingness to tell me stories at all times. I was always torn between the Chicago Fire and duck-hunting on the Calumet marshes as the source of his narrative. We would know very much less about Chicago's appearance before the fire were it not for this pioneer photographer, nor without him would we have the magnificent smooth-faced, profiled portrait of Lincoln.

To describe Hesler's panorama would be but to repeat much of our description of the "Bird's-Eye View" except that the churches had commenced their flight from Washington Street where Mammon threatened their sanctuaries and also that the newer commercial buildings were beginning to show bracketed cornices and other architectural furbelows, advanced agents of the new fashions in architecture. We are also indebted to this pioneer photographer for his splendid daguerreotype of the old City Hall taken on Independence Day, 1855. Long John Wentworth is on the ground to the right of the steps delivering a patriotic oration and the adolescent city is standing on the threshold of its manhood. As a farewell to childhood, what is more eloquent than a paragraph in the *Annual Review* of the commerce of Chicago written in 1854? "Speaking of fast changing Chicago we are forcibly reminded of the figure of a young and beautiful damsel whose rounding form and budding proportions are fast bursting from the limited and straining vestments which sufficed her girlhood and demanding a costume of more flowing dimensions and costly texture."

The principal architects of Chicago at the turning of the ways in 1855 were: Carter and Bauer at 51 and 53 LaSalle; William W. Boyington at 12 Dearborn; Burling and Baumann in the Marine Bank Building at the corner of La Salle and Lake; Otto H. Matz at 84 Dearborn; E. Willard Smith in the Exchange Building, at the corner of

From Andreas, "History of Chicago," Vol. I

THE SECOND CHICAGO COURT HOUSE, JOHN M. VAN OSDEL, ARCHITECT, 1853

Lake and Clark; and Van Osdel and Olmstead at 16 Dearborn. The amount of work that these architects performed seems incredible. While many of these buildings, gleaned from the reports of the *Annual Review,* were insignificant, to offset them there were blocks of stores and houses and many were important operations. Of the buildings reported as building in this year, Carter and Bauer had 32 houses, 1 church and 13 commercial structures; Boyington, 17 houses, 1 church and 7 commercial; Burling and Baumann, 1 house, 1 church, 12 commercial, 1 public, and 3 hotels; Matz had 2 houses, 1 school, and 2 commercial; Van Osdel had 19 houses, 10 commercial, 3 hotels and 2 schools; Olmstead and Nicholson had 11 houses, 1 church, 5 commercial, 1 school.

Nor does this include out-of-town work of which Carter and Bauer had eight jobs, mostly houses; Smith had five; Burling and Bauer had five, mostly public and commercial; Otto Matz had four including railway stations for the Illinois Central, a railroad hotel and the court house at Kankakee; Van Osdel had thirteen including "Old College," Northwestern University, court houses at LaPorte, Morris and Woodstock. Matz had six out-of-town buildings, including court house at Bourbonnais, a country seat at Lake Geneva, churches, etc. Olmstead and Nicholson seemed to specialize in out-of-town work with a $50,000 church in Kankakee, a court in Belvidere, a hotel in Rockford and eight other important commissions.

CHAPTER III

Growing Pains · 1855-1880

IT is not a pleasant thing to an architect to realize that in the thirties, forties, and fifties the builder, left to himself, his tools and his handbook, built houses, churches, and other simple structures that posterity has proclaimed very good, but that when the professional architect in the later fifties, sixties, and seventies entered the scene, particularly in the Middle West, the buildings that were created have become a byword and were useful apparently only as horrible examples. The reasons were simple enough. The architects of those times were presumably intelligent men, certainly possessed of exuberant energy and unabashed confidence, and they did their best; but they were not trained in the present sense, when four years or more in a school of architecture seems to be a prerequisite. Few of them had ever been abroad, which would have been particularly valuable at this time as they and their clients had chosen for their dish the most highly flavored and indigestible styles that Europe had produced to date. If, then, we are convinced that this architecture of Chicago which succeeded the Greek Revival and continued to the Chicago Fire and, as a matter of fact, considerably later, was not notable for its taste, architectural beauty or suitability, these convictions were most certainly not shared by the city's boosters and citizens of the time, for they acclaimed Chicago the most wonderful city in the world and her architecture as handsome as any of the land, a fitting expression for the miracle of her existence.

Critics have a very dangerous but prevalent habit of adding merit to the mode they are championing by attacking a previous mode. This is also true of the champions of the streamline style of today, well called the International Style, with whom it is usually the Renaissance or some form of Classic architecture that becomes the scapegoat. Human intelligence doesn't vary from age to age. The only advantage we have over our ancestors is that of experience and the use of the store of things that accumulate through the ages. While, therefore, it cannot well be assumed that the people who did thus and so, let us say in architecture, did it in the best possible way, we may safely conclude that their art justly expressed the culture that produced it. One thing is certain, if you and I had lived in that particular time we should have done as they did. It is especially dangerous to condemn an aboriginal art, crude as it may seem, for there is a chance that in its force, directness and truth it may be great art. In other words, the only fair way to judge a work of art or architecture of a previous time is not by comparing it with the best of this day, but with the best of its own time. Are we, therefore, on dangerous ground in maligning the architecture of Chicago, as practiced from the middle eighteen-fifties to almost 1880? Did they or did they not know what they were doing? And the answer to that is, in my opinion, that they did not. For when we use our formula and compare it with the best of its time not only in England and France but in some of our eastern cities, we see how very bad it was.

To be retrospective again, several architectural styles or periods had preceded this in America. Let's boil them down to two: the Colonial and Post-Colonial from about 1700 to 1820, and the Greek Revival from 1820 to 1850. Both of these were decidedly superior according to our rule to our Parvenu period from 1855 to 1880. There were, however, sufficient reasons. Our Colonial, though inspired by the contemporary Georgian of England, ran a course of more than one hundred years, in which it developed an American technique guided by a high level of general taste; besides, its problems were simple and in general its buildings small. In its successor, the Greek Revival, the problem was still simple and the buildings for the most part small, and though there were few architects the builder got exactly what he wanted from his excellent handbook. Moreover, though the Greek mania seems to us not only exotic but ridiculous, its simplicity and directness in the hands of the pioneer builder and the rare architect resulted in structures that are almost always pleasing and at least more than half-way convincing. About 1855, however, conditions changed tremendously. The extension of the railroads and the development of natural resources introduced big business into every American city. The first requirements were large and complex buildings, among which were the first office buildings. Five and even six stories were the usual heights and the technique of structure with efforts at fire-proofing became more and more complicated. Great buildings were being erected in London and Paris and naturally, as before, we turned to them for guidance. Most unhappily for us, the prevailing fashions in those emporiums of taste were rich and sophisticated, so much so that even the European architects, trained and brilliant as they were, had trouble in keeping their fractious styles in hand. In the surge of

Fashion that brought what I have called the Parvenu period of Architecture upon us our merchant princes and their wives were possibly more to blame than our eager but unprepared architects. Someone should write a volume on the mighty force of Fashion.

Perhaps it is not out of my province to say that the attitude of those twenty-five years toward life, appearance and manners smacked of the Parvenu as well. At no time was dress more uncomfortable and, in the sense of concealing the human form, more ridiculous, nor had prudery ever masked human emotions so successfully, snobbery been so admired, the world so sure of itself. The art of this period—that for instance of the Hudson River School and Rogers Groups, relegated to the attic at the time of the World's Fair of 1893—has not yet emerged. It takes a hundred years to create an antique; so it may yet come into its own. Never had the pocket-book such a power to open doors to either parlor or forum, and never had art and architecture so venal a standard. In contrast, and every age abounds in contrasts, the literature of Whitman, Hawthorne, Emerson and Longfellow yielded but little to the England of Browning's day, and at no other time had the fire to redress wrong, free the slave, maintain liberty and spread the gospel of Christianity throughout the world burned more brightly.

Energy, like courage, remains about constant through the ages, and from 1855 to 1880 it was responsible for a vast industrial development in this country. An important part of it was the boom in trans-Atlantic travel. The first steamship crossed the ocean from Cork to New York in 1839, but sailing vessels continued to be the principal means of transportation until the fifties. The Great Eastern, the wonder of her time, though an economic failure, at least made Americans travel-conscious in the sense of travel for pleasure and in safety. The fifties brought the screw propeller; the sixties, the compound engine; the seventies, comforts for the passengers; and the eighties, the steel hull. You may be sure, therefore, that the above-mentioned merchant princes, their alert wives and their pretty daughters had their eyes open when they stood awestruck in the Crystal Palace, walked along Regent Street or drove through the Champs Elysées. What they found as the latest architectural fashions in England was the work of a coterie of brilliant young architects who, under Augustus A. W. Pugin first and later John Ruskin, had staged a direct assault on the old Classic or Greek Revival and had proposed as a national style, instead, a Gothic Revival. This struggle is known in the history of Architecture as the Battle of the Styles. The Crystal Palace of 1851, smoldering in ruin as I write these words, epitomized the glories of the young Victoria's happy reign and marked the triumph as well of the Gothic Revival in the Battle of the Styles.

About 1860 the Gothic Revival in England took on an Italian hue, owing to the eloquent preaching of Ruskin, who in his "Stones of Venice" raised Venetian architecture to the empyrean. Such was the situation in England. Across the channel equally lusty forces were busy reshaping the course of architecture. Napoleon the Third ascended the throne of France in 1852 and his Empress Eugénie, the throne of Fashion. As in the case of Victoria, the architects of Napoleon believed that a burgeoning Golden Age should be fitly framed in a new architecture, and proceeded to evolve an extremely rich and sophisticated style. This was, however, not something entirely novel as in England, but a richly varied form of the Renaissance that the French have stuck to since the early sixteenth century. Of many examples the two outstanding are the Opera House in Paris, begun in 1861, and a new wing of the Louvre.

Such, then, was the lay influence on our architecture of the sixties and seventies, but it did not by any means whitewash our architects, for a building, as it should be, is always a game of give and take between architect and client. In the east Robert Ware, Richard M. Hunt and James Renwick had built the Art Museum in Boston, the Lenox Library in New York, and St. Patrick's Cathedral in New York respectively, all excellent buildings, and there were a few others. But it was in the Middle West that the styles so furiously raged together, and particularly in Chicago that the architects imagined a vain thing. The reason was our complete unpreparedness.

If at the time we had had a large number of architects, instead of a very few, trained in knowledge of the styles at architectural schools and with taste developed by European travel and first-hand knowledge of the buildings that they admired so much, the story would have been different. But for better or worse we must take them as they are or were. Since elaboration was a *sine qua non* of the buildings of the day and haste always of the essence, the architect was doubly dependent on inspiration from without. This inspiration, in that day as in this, was usually, first, what the other fellow was doing and second, one's own ideas, if any. The Chicago libraries containing most of the architectural history of this period were destroyed by the Great Fire, and I have been unable to find any lists of their contents. But we have lists of libraries in other cities. Mr. Russell Hitchcock has supplied me with one of the library of the great H. H. Richardson of Boston. Though the name of Richardson is associated with the succeeding phase of architectural fashion, still he started practice in 1865, and so his library must have been in some degree typical. It contains among about one hundred listed works the following: Ruskin; Pugin, virtually father of the Gothic Revival; Britton, *Architectural Antiquities of Great Britain;* Burgess, *Architectural Drawings* (1870) —an Englishman, idol of the draughting-room; Gaillabaud, with a monumental work on Architecture from the fifth to the seventeenth centuries; Latarouilly, whose *Edifices of Modern Rome* (1856-60) was the supreme authority then as now; Nash, *Mansions of England in the Olden Time;* Sauvageot, *Palais, Chateaux, Hôtels et Maisons de France* (1872), and Viollet-le-Duc, authority on the philosophy of architecture and the restorer of Pierrefonds and Carcassonne. Contemporary buildings like the Crystal Palace, churches by Street, Scott and Burgess in England—all eminent Victorians—the Paris Opéra, Bibliothèque Ste. Geneviève and additions to the Louvre would not yet be included in standard works but were familiar in periodicals and in the newly developed and highly popular craft of the photographer. In Richardson's library we find photographs of the work of many of the great Victorians, but curiously none of contemporary French buildings, even of the Louvre, on which he worked himself.[1] John Root as a boy thumbed a volume of Lefèvre which his father gave him.

The principal foreign architectural periodicals of the day with the dates of their first volumes are: *The Archi-*

[1] *The Builder,* London, 1861, mentions among others the following books recommended to the young architect:
Brandon—*Analysis of Gothic Architecture*
Chambers—*Treatise on the Decorative Part of Civil Architecture*
Fergusson—*Hand Book of Architecture*
Hittorf—*L'Architecture Polychrome*
Latarouilly—*Edifices de Rome Modern*
Palladio—*Buildings and Designs*
Pugin—*True Principles of Pointed or Christian Architecture*
Repton—*Landscape Gardening and Landscape Architecture*
Rickman—*An Attempt To Discriminate the Styles of English Architecture*
Vitruvius—*Architecture,* etc.

tect, London, 1849; *Architectural Association Sketch Book,* London, 1867; *British Architect,* 1874; *Building News and Engineering Journal,* 1854; *Croquis d'Architecture,* 1866; *Deutsche Bau Zeitung,* Berlin, 1867; *Allgemeine Bau Zeitung,* Vienna, 1826. Doubtless the more important Chicago architects subscribed to some of these.[2]

The early volumes of these magazines contained comparatively few illustrations; wood-cuts were expensive, but it is significant that the cuts were highly diversified and divided roughly into equal parts—contemporary native work, contemporary foreign work, and ancient work. Among the illustrations in Volume I of *The Builder*[3] are: Gilbert Scott's famous Town Hall at Halifax (England); Walton Hall in the Gothic style also by Scott; Schools at Lambeth by J. L. Pearson (Gothic with Italian touches); Pugin's Gothic Cathedral of St. Thomas the Apostle at Northampton; Barry's design, in his Italianate style, for a proposed new National Gallery in London; various French houses showing mansard roofs, *Néo-Grec* detail and incised ornaments; the design for famous St. Michael's Fountain, Paris; many illustrations of mediaeval architecture, such as Melrose Abbey, Westminster Abbey, etc. The 1862 volume contains illustrations and a description of Butterfield's St. Alban's Church, a veritable treasure trove to our church architects of the day, and then comes a series of Albert Memorials and our cue for putting the dusty and rickety tomes back on their shelves.

---

[2] American Architectural magazines of the time were: *American Architect and Builder's Monthly,* 1870-71; *American Builder,* 1870-79; *American Builder and Journal of Art,* 1869; *Architectural Sketch Book,* 1873-76; *New York Sketch Book,* 1874-76; Sloan's *Architectural Review and Builder's Journal,* 1869-70; Woodward's *Architecture.*

[3] The first number of this weekly magazine appeared December 31, 1842.

Perhaps I am too verbose in the matter of sources, but it seems to me that it is very important to ascertain how our architects of the sixties and seventies "got that way," especially if we are disposed to be harsh with them. There was one other source and this was the plan books, ungainly and raucous offspring of the sedate handbooks of the forties and fifties, from whose engraved leaves popped the Greek Revival. These plan books were not intended to slip into the breeches pocket of a carpenter, but to be spread out on the marble-topped walnut table of an architect or owner.

The styles they promoted show an extraordinary uniformity from one book to another and are so close to the buildings of the period that one wonders which was the chicken and which the egg. In *Architectural Designs for Street Fronts, Suburban Houses and Cottages* by Cummings and Miller, 1872 (I am examining the eighth edition, so it must have been popular), one finds almost all the features we associate with buildings of the period— a real Parvenu Bible: jig saw brackets, called in those days "trusses"—several I recognize as stemming from the Paris Opéra; ornamental brick cornices for commercial buildings, one of the good features of the period; cast-iron shop fronts, still to be found occasionally, as on Lake Street, but everywhere then; façades of banking houses and insurance offices showing the typical arrangement of the first floor five or six feet above the sidewalk level and the remaining stories of superimposed orders divided by intermediate cornices; the details, coarse French or Italian; all are here.

In this book there is also a Gothic office-building of the Ruskin-Italianate variety, much better, as is usual, than the Classic or Renaissance designs. Many details of mansard roofs, verge boards and gable ends, window caps, piazzas, observatories (cupolas to us), newel-posts and balustrades, dormer windows, etc., abound. A large book with colored plates entitled *Architectural Designs for Model Country Houses* by John Riddle, 1864, has many familiar types. His houses are squarish, of smooth stucco, each with a cupola and a heavy cornice with the scroll-sawed brackets. They tie up with the previous Greek Revival in their friezes with "Attic" windows and their low tin roofs. There are a number with cast-iron trellises. The author says in his introduction that his houses "are in a style which has never been attempted in this country or Europe." The plans are very poor, and never is there more than one bath to the entire house. Most of the drawings are from houses already executed.

A book of much better quality is *Church Architecture* by H. H. Holly, 1871, dedicated significantly to George Edmund Street, the distinguished English Gothicist of the time (the man who did the famous Law Courts in London). He gives us many an enlightening point in his introduction: "Perpendicular Gothic is decrepit and decadent," and he objects to its smooth walls; "At this time in this country a strong movement is going on in favor of Italian Gothic"; "Not a single attempt at an American style has so far shown itself"; he strongly objects to a square ended chancel and prefers the rounded apse; and he naïvely remarks that he disapproves of "Victorian Gothic, as it is sometimes called," because it is "quaint and bizarre." Nevertheless, his designs are all Victorian Gothic of the deepest dye and with a strong Ruskinian tinge. In quality they were far superior to any church architecture being done in Chicago.

Holly also published in 1863 (written in 1859) a book called *Country Seats*. Although an educated man, he expresses a common view of the time that is incomprehensible to us today. He shows an early Colonial house, simple and beautiful in its proportion and fenestration, and alongside he depicts how it could be remodelled into a "Modern Villa." He says of the Colonial house "that it is devoid of beauty, grace or expression, pinched and contracted in all its features, ceilings are low—rooms small: green wood shutters 'adorn' the windows and the outer walls if painted at all are of glaring white," yet, he adds in apparent astonishment, "Within the shadow of the humblest of these have been born and reared some of the most distinguished men of our history." What were the principal buildings of the Chicago that were almost obliterated but that once stood so self-confidently in the hot southwest winds during the summer of 1871? Still dominating the city sky-line was the combined city and county building generally known as the "Court House," but, like the court house of many another town, it had undergone some devastating changes. Not only had the city and county outgrown the excellent buildings that Van Osdel erected in 1853, but its Greek Revival style was no longer modish, so only a year before the Fire two great wings were added to the east and to the west, a third story was built over all, and the whole surmounted by a giant cupola. The round-headed windows with keystones, the heavy bracketed cornice, the curved pediments, and the huge stone urns proclaimed that Van Osdel had mounted the band wagon and was giving the city the last word in the French style, at least as he understood it. Even its contemporaries admitted "it lacked unity." One of these stone urns, or more properly finials, stood for years in front of the old Avenue House in Evanston. The original building was constructed of limestone from the Lockport, New York, quarries, and the additions were of limestone from the Lemont quarries in Cook County unsmilingly referred to as "Athens marble" by the boosters. Views of the ruins show little to choose from between the two in fire resistance. The fire left nothing but gaunt walls, but it must be remembered that it stood in the axis of the conflagration as it swept the city.

The Federal Building, housing customs and post-office, stood at the northwest corner of Dearborn and Monroe. This building was interesting because it was typical of such structures designed by the government architect in Washington at that time. Contemporary Federal buildings that I have observed in St. Louis and Galena are almost identical except for size. These buildings were designed in a very restrained Roman-Classic style with stories of ample round-arched windows and strongly divided by horizontal belt cornices, the whole crowned by a bold cornice correctly detailed. The upper stories were smooth, but the first was rusticated, that is, there were deep grooves along the line of the jointing.

As one reads over old accounts of Chicago buildings in pre-Fire days, hotels, churches and theatres seem to call for the most attention; office-buildings were much in the background. The best of these last named were to be found along State, Dearborn, Clark and LaSalle, and their cross streets Lake, Washington, Madison and Monroe. Business was rapidly encroaching on Wabash Avenue and Michigan, and the residences and churches for some time had been retreating to quieter quarters. While the names of many a church, store and bank persist to the present day, those of the office-buildings or "blocks," as they were called, seem strange and unfamiliar. The Bryan, the Arcade, the Boone, the Bowen, Cobb's, Dickey's, Fullerton's, Garrett's, Link's, McCarthy's, Magies', Union, and then several with a friendly ring, Honoré, Otis, Scammon and the Portland Block. All of these "blocks" were in the central district described above. On the North Side two important ones were the Purple on Ontario and Clark and the Uhlich on Clark near Kinzie.

The early chronicles of Chicago reflect the pride of the growing city in her hotels. Only forty-one years elapsed from Wolf Tavern, 1830, to the grand new Palmer House, waiting for its roof when the Fire pre-empted every room, but in that time some fifteen to twenty hotels of importance had been built. The Sherman House, the Grand Pacific, the Tremont House, the Palmer House were institutions. Every one of them had been rebuilt, the Sherman and the Tremont several times, but in each case the last rebuilding was in the decade previous to the Fire. The French Renaissance fashion of the day was just the dish for the big hotels. The new wings of the Louvre and the Grand Hotels of the boulevards answered all the questions. There were the great pavilion in the center for the grand entrance and the corner pavilions just for looks; there were the high, wide and handsome intermediate stories for the bedrooms, and there were the mansard roofs, sometimes two stories in height, for the cheap rooms and the servants. The broad façades occupying important corners offered unlimited opportunity for architectural embellishment. The three orders, Doric, Ionic, Corinthian, with their respective entablatures were called upon for heavy duty: stone balconies at strategic points; sculpture and caryatids for opulent effects; and, crowning the roofs over the pavilions, domes in the approved Parisian mode. Perhaps the multitude of chimneys, many with pots and extensions to improve the draught (I can count twenty-six along the two façades of the Sherman House), gave the truest Parisian touch. My belief is that these great pre- and post-Fire buildings with their legitimate architectural display exerted the controlling influences in commercial architecture.

The huge Sherman House (1861) at Clark and Randolph streets was built with plain walls of Athens marble and a strong cornice. The Palmer House (1869-70) on the northwest corner of State and Quincy streets, had comparatively plain walls, but a huge French mansard roof. The Grand Pacific Hotel, at Clark, Jackson, La Salle and Quincy, "a magnificent structure six stories in height built in the modern Italian style with four grand entrances," died aborning, for it was caught in the holocaust of '71 before it opened its doors. But according to Andreas it left "an imposing and beautiful ruin." One hopes that that was some consolation. The long-forgotten Bigelow House on the southwest corner of Dearborn and Adams, a tragedy of the building boom that preceded the Fire, was a high building "in the German style" and cost nearly a half million. Its grand opening was scheduled for October 9, 1871, but the only guests were the flames that devoured the roses, lapped up the punch and ruined the proprietors. The Briggs House (1853) was an old timer on the northeast corner of Randolph and Wells. The rebuilt hotel lasted until 1926. Of all the post-Fire relics it looked the most ancient, and I always suspected that it was rebuilt from the original plans. The hotel with the most personality seems to have been the Tremont House. The original Tremont House was built in 1832 at the northwest corner of Lake and Dearborn streets, but its successor, number three, was erected in 1850 on the southeast corner of Lake and Dearborn. The *Gem of the Prairie* in January, 1851, has this to say of it: "The Tremont House has precedence of all others. It is one of the chief ornaments of the city and reflects great credit on its proprietor, Mr. Ira Couch. The house is five and a half stories high and its internal arrangements, including furniture and decorations, are all in the highest style of art, and of the class denominated princely. There is perhaps no hotel in the Union superior to it in any respect. The cost of the building was $75,000; J. M. Van Osdel, architect and superintendent." If the *Gem of the Prairie* is correct, the building cost only five cents per cubic foot. The lone tomb which still stands near the south end of Lincoln Park and arouses curiosity or moralizing contains the body of this intrepid pioneer as well as those of his father and his two sons, who, strangely enough, had moved to Cuba shortly before he died in 1857.

Of theaters, there was McVicker's built in 1857 and remodelled about 1870. The architecture, striking as it was with its two square cupolas on the corners was over-shadowed, as often happens, by the personalities which occupied it. Murdoch, Edwin Booth, J. Wilkes Booth, Gottschalk, Lotta Crabtree, Barrett, Joseph Jefferson crossed its boards, but to me all yield place in romantic appeal to Mary McVicker, who after months of pleading got her father's consent to play Juliet opposite Edwin Booth's Romeo. She was eighteen at the time, and this fairy tale appearance was an ovation. She won not only Chicago and New York audiences but her Romeo as well, for she became Mrs. Booth the following year.

A building that pops up into the ken of any student of old Chicago is Crosby's Opera House. As Andreas says: "The history of this famous temple of art is one without a parallel in the west. Its enormous cost, its elegance of design, its vicissitudes as a financial investment, its brief existence, its devotion to grand operatic and dramatic uses" raise it in interest above the level of any other theater in the West. Uranus H. Crosby, wealthy distiller, knowing nothing about the theater but convinced that

Burke and Koretke photograph from Joseph T. Ryerson Collection

THE GRAND PACIFIC HOTEL, OF 1872, CLARK, JACKSON, LASALLE, AND QUINCY STREETS

Famous for its "Hunter's Dinners"

CROSBY'S OPERA HOUSE, W. W. BOYINGTON, ARCHITECT

On Washington Street before the fire

Chicago needed a palace of opera and art, put his entire fortune, $600,000, into the enterprise and regarded it as lost before the opening night. This opening was inauspicious. The assassination of President Lincoln postponed it for several months and after dramatic vicissitudes, during which it was won in a famous raffle for $5 and resold to Crosby for $200,000, it came to the inevitable fiery end the night of the proposed opening of the season by Theodore Thomas and his orchestra of sixty. The building was called Italian in style though it boasted the fashionable mansard roof. Its main feature was a triumphal arch supporting statuary representing the arts. A magnifying glass discloses on the woodcut the still familiar names in the business of music—W. W. Kimball, Bauer and Company, and Root and Cady. Its location was on the north side of Washington, between State and Dearborn.

Other show-houses that went up in smoke were the famous Wood's Museum on Randolph Street, a combination of theater, dime museum and art gallery. One could see *East Lynne,* inspect the celebrated Zeuglodon, fossil monster ninety-six feet long, or shudder over the hand-painted masterpiece, "The Murder of Jane McRae"—all under the same roof. Other amusement halls of the sixties of more interest to the histrionic historian than the architect were Hooley's, Aiken's Museum, Dearborn Theatre, Metropolitan Hall, etc.

When one attempts to describe the churches which in every direction punctured Chicago's otherwise level silhouette on the eve of the Fire, one trembles at the task, for this was the heyday of aggressive Christianity and the multiplication of her temples. Perhaps if one mentions but one or two of each denomination in addition to all that has been said before it will suffice.

The pioneer churches in the Greek Revival style with

porticos and pediments and often with belfries and steeples were short-lived both in fashion and in usefulness and for the most part made way for fast encroaching business. They have already been described. The Gothic Revival in England, which triumphed over the Classic about 1850 in the Battle of the Styles, set the fashion in no uncertain way in the States. There certainly was not a single Classic edifice among the churches built in Chicago after 1857. All were Gothic or called so at least. Almost all were of rock face Joliet limestone and almost all were of a singularly thin and unattractive design. The problem of designing the façade of a Christian church, so easily and gracefully solved by the French, but a stumbling block to the English even in the thirteenth and fourteenth centuries at the height of the Gothic style, seemed to be passed along to our grandfathers with far worse results. In fact, today with all our knowledge and accumulated skill it is still one of the most difficult that the architect has to meet. With only one or two exceptions, when a sort of round-arched Gothic—one can hardly call it Romanesque—style was used, every one of the multitude of churches built between 1850 and the Fire was in the Gothic fashion. Two types were used—either the Mediaeval English styles of the thirteenth and fourteenth centuries (Early English and Decorated) or else the Victorian Gothic which had in its latter phases a strong Italian tinge. This Italian tinge came from the eloquence of John Ruskin and the profound influence of his *Stones of Venice* and was interpreted in England by men like Butterfield, Burgess and Scott. Undoubtedly, churches like All Saints or St. Albans in London encouraged us in our license in turning our naves and chancels into bedlams of senseless frescoes and bad glass.

To return for a minute to the earlier fashion of Mediaeval Gothic, George Edmund Street in England was interpreting it in many modern buildings such as Bristol Cathedral and the Law Courts in London. We can probably put our finger on the work of Street more than that of any other influence as the "nigger in the wood pile" of our ecclesiastical design of the ten years on either side of the Fire.

Baffled by the number of churches destroyed by the Fire, let us mention only one or two of each denomination. Standing this minute on Roosevelt Road near May is the group of the Church of the Holy Family. The church, with a very picturesque tower, French in character, was built in 1857. The priests' house on the west was built in 1862, and the large school building, also by the Jesuits, to the east, was erected in 1864. Here is a rare group of pre-Fire buildings unscathed by flame or alteration. Old St. Stephen's, with a grotto on West Twenty-second Place, is yet more interesting. It was built in 1853 and is so early that though it pretends to Gothic it still has a few fragments of its Greek Revival shell stuck to its feathers. The great building of Catholicism then as now, however, was the Cathedral of the Holy Name. The original building on its site on the northeast corner of State and Superior was rather different from the present edifice, for though monumental in size it was constructed of brick, and the high tower was in the center. When first erected in 1854 it stood almost at the northern limit of the city.

St. James' of the Episcopal diocese comes in time and again for mention. The church as it now stands, southeast corner of Huron and Wabash, is a rebuilding of the one erected in 1857 for the most part, though the tower and façade were added in '68 and the church consecrated by Bishop Whitehouse in 1864. A comparison of an old woodcut and a present photograph shows the tower to be identical but the main west window to have been redesigned. The style is Early English. Under an account of the architect, Edward Burling, something more will be said about it.

One should perhaps mention Grace, built in 1867, being on Wabash Avenue near 14th. It escaped the Big Fire, but not one that destroyed it in 1915. Its façade of Athens marble was a wild but vigorous interpretation of Early English Gothic. The portal was outrageous but the spire appears interesting. Its successor by Bertram Goodhue was also destroyed by fire, and the third in succession, built by this author, stands next to St. Luke's Hospital.

The New England Church of the Congregationalists, 1863, had more interest and personality than most of its day. Perhaps it was the two pillars of Scotch marble that flanked the crude but powerful portal, perhaps it was the gigantic Peterborough-like arch that almost filled the façade. More likely, it was the historic stones, that, like sculptured saints, occupied elaborate Gothic niches above the portal. One was from "Scrooby Manor A.D. 1606," another "Delft Haven 1620," whence the Pilgrims sailed, and another "Plymouth Rock December 22, 1620." The interior woodwork was black walnut, a favorite in Chicago of pre-Fire churches that had plenty of money. Its location on the southeast corner of Delaware (White in those days) and Dearborn insured its destruction, but when rebuilt a good deal of the old stone-work was left, showing the teeth of the fire, as does St. James.' In the rebuilding the transepts were extended in an interesting polygonal form. The New England Church was a center of missionary zeal among the Congregationalists. Fire has been its nemesis. On July 14, 1936, the reconstructed church burned again and this time the site was cleared.

From "History of St. James' Church, Chicago," 1934

THE RUINS OF ST. JAMES' EPISCOPAL CHURCH
EDWARD BURLING, ARCHITECT, 1857

After the fire

From "History of St. James' Church," 1934

ST. JAMES' EPISCOPAL CHURCH, WABASH AVENUE
AND HURON STREET

As rebuilt in 1875

Plymouth Church, equally prosperous, was built in 1865 on the corner of Madison and Dearborn at a cost of $100,000. We read that in 1871 an organ was installed at a cost of $10,000, just in time, of course, to go up in flames.

At the time of the Fire the Presbyterians were rich in churches. Always at the head of the list was the First Church, the descendant, you will remember, of the Reverend Jeremiah Porter's sermon in Fort Dearborn in 1833. This church stood on Wabash Avenue between Van Buren and Congress and was erected in 1856-57 at a cost of $115,000. It was of rock-faced Athens marble. It is described as of "the Norman style of architecture, the front highly ornamented and richly carved," [4] and in truth the windows were round-arched, but the high "lanterns" or belfries on the two towers, the pinnacles and buttresses are all Gothic.

As famous as the First was the Second. This has been described as the *chef d'oeuvre* of Van Osdel, known from the bituminous excrescences of the limestone as the "Spotted Church" or the "Church of the Holy Zebra." [5]

The Methodist losses were not so great. Trinity, Michigan Avenue near Twenty-second, dedicated by my grandfather in 1864,[6] survived until 1917. Grace, however, on the northwest corner of LaSalle and Chicago Avenue, where Moody Institute now stands, was completely destroyed. A cut of the ruins shows the universal rock-face Joliet limestone and the pinched Gothic detail. The Wabash Avenue Methodist Church, Fourteenth Street and Wabash, was a survivor and a mute hero of the Fire. Here the flames were stopped on their southward progress and in the old church built in 1857 the Post-Office took

---

[4] Andreas, *History of Chicago,* I, 302.

[5] *Ibid,* II, 417.

[6] Rev. Thomas M. Eddy.

refuge. The church had a homely but honest flat face with a small tower in the pasteboard Gothic of the time and seems to have been built of brick.

A place to study ante- and post-Fire church architecture is at the southeast corner of Walton Place and Dearborn Street where stands Unity Church, now a consistory of the Scottish Rite but famous in those days and for long after as the pulpit of Robert Collyer. He it was who at the call of Father Abraham threw a great American flag over his pulpit and announced to his congregation, "This place is closed, I'm going to the War." As he did. Unity is the handiwork of Collyer. You can still decipher on the cornerstone "Anno Domini 1867." A great deal of the original building remains—the main entrance, the lower part of the towers and portions of the side walls. The new great window follows the old design, but the two small identical steeples were changed to the present great spire and lesser one. We could go on and describe St. Paul's Universalist on the corner of Wabash and Van Buren, a handsome French Gothic church reduced to a shell by the fire, the four or five German Evangelical Churches, the synagogues, etc., but haven't we had enough?

While the good old stand-bys like Andreas' *Chicago* are voluble and even eloquent in churches and hotels, they are strangely silent on the dwelling-houses that sheltered our hearthstones in the decade before the Fire. By that time the Greek Revival houses that once lined Wabash Avenue and Michigan had long since been driven out by business, but fine houses had sprung up in the north division along Pine and the neighboring streets as far as the Catholic Cemetery, which extended from Schiller to North Avenue. Rufus Blanchard's map of 1867 [7] gives us many a surprise. Pine Street, now Michigan

[7] Chicago Historical Society.

THE SECOND PRESBYTERIAN CHURCH, THE "SPOTTED" CHURCH,
WABASH AVENUE AND WASHINGTON STREET

THE MAHLON B. OGDEN HOUSE, BUILT ON THE NEWBERRY LIBRARY SITE

A lonely survivor of the fire

Avenue, ran into the Lake near Whitney Street, the ancient name for Walton; familiar Delaware was White; Bellevue was Oakwood; while Goethe was yclept Grand.

In the decade before the Fire almost all traces of the Greek Revival had disappeared. There are very few buildings in Chicago that show us how the new style supplanted the old, although there are many examples in the smaller towns and in the country-side of Northern Illinois and Southern Wisconsin that illustrate this evolution of one fashion into another. As a matter of fact, it was not truly an evolution. The Parvenu architecture of the sixties and seventies did not "evolve" from the pioneer Greek Revival style of the forties. What happened was that one after another of the dignified features of the pioneer buildings were abandoned for some feature that the builder fondly thought was stylish abroad and knew was stylish at home. The sequence of the disappearing Greek Revival was something like this. The square or oblong body of the building persisted for some time while its simple habiliments were being yanked off and replaced with something more stylish and far more showy. Free-standing Greek columns were so rare that they need hardly be considered, but in the ordinary house the little returns of the cornice at the gable ends, so characteristic of the pioneer house, were first abandoned. Next, the chaste Classic cornice, or what there was left of it, was replaced by a heavy over-hanging cornice with the scroll-sawn brackets. Then, the corner pilasters, which had been getting thinner and thinner, lost their caps and bases and became mere corner boards or, if on brick buildings, disappeared altogether. In the meantime, elaborate scroll-sawed verandas were supplanting the simple stoops or columned porches. There was a vast amount of variety in these verandas, and some of them were not without beauty or at least charm. This is especially true of the later ones in the "cottage style," where moldings were eliminated and the scroll-sawn supports took a vast variety of shapes, often following graceful motives of vines and branches. As changing fashions came on apace, ceilings were heightened, windows grew high and narrow and their heads were often arched. These window heads were usually crowned with a heavy molded cap. Exterior blinds largely disappeared in favor of interior shutters that cleverly folded into receptacles in the window jambs. With the high basement, elaborate chimney and cupola, the last to be developed, the house of the sixties and seventies had thrown off all resemblance to its simple and dignified predecessor—hardly progenitor. Even in the old towns of Lake View and Hyde Park examples of pre-Fire houses are hard to find.

Such a house as we have described was that of George F. Rumsey on the corner of Rush and Huron streets. Destroyed by the Fire, we can confidently depend on an old woodcut.[8] The high basement, the high narrow porch, the huge bracketed cornice, and the great square cupola, the device of the merchant prince, all run true to form. This cupola-ed form of house with surrounding porches was particularly popular in the suburbs—in Hyde Park, Kenwood, Lake View and Evanston. The Mahlon D. Ogden house, famous as having alone on the North Side been overlooked by the Fire, followed more nearly the French tradition in that it proudly displayed a full mansard roof, and appears from the photograph to have been well designed.

There was also the brick gabled residence of H. H. Magie, father of Mrs. Lambert Tree, occupying a full block between Ohio and Ontario, east of State, where the Tree

[8] Chamberlain, *Chicago and Its Suburbs,* 1874.

Studio Building now stands. It is described as being "brick gabled" and "full of beautiful things brought from abroad." [9] On the northeast corner of State and Ontario stood the "dark brown cottage" of the George B. Meekers. Another great house occupying a block directly east of the Ogdens was that of Walter N. Newberry, whose fortune founded the Newberry Library. Julia Newberry in her delightful diary tells of the direful news of the destruction of the family mansion in the Fire, as read in a letter in a European spa. The house was brown stone, we know that much. The General Joseph Stockton dwelling stood on the southeast corner of Rush and Ohio and opposite was that of George E. Stanton. North of the Newberrys was the Arnold house, which is described as a large one with a basement dining-room. Dr. Brainard had a "Milwaukee brick" house on the corner of Rush and Huron, and also nearby on Huron were the homes of the Rumseys, one of which has been described. Opposite Washington Square was the residence of Ezra B. McCagg, "the handsomest in Chicago." [10] This occupied two blocks and contained a "large stately library" with books to the ceiling.

Up to twenty years ago those of us who commuted on the Elevated could ruminate on the past glories of "Buena House," the James B. Waller home which stood, deserted and forlorn, in what was once a splendid estate on Evanston Avenue in Lake View. This huge house, which cost $75,000 in days when building was less than half of now, followed the formula of the time, including the cupola, in that case, a huge one. Mr. Samuel B. Chase, who came to Chicago in 1850 and became an expert in abstracts and real estate, had his home on a ten-acre lot on Belden Avenue, for which he paid $70 per acre. His

[9] Kirkland, *Chicago's Yesterdays*, Mary Drummond's account.
[10] *Ibid.*, p. 131.

house, very attractive in the old woodcut, was one-story with a high mansard. S. H. Kerfoot, who built his famous real estate shed on the smoking embers of the Fire, also lived in a house of the "cottage type." Kerfoot "will soon build an unequaled homestead in his large and exquisite grounds extending to the lake." [11]

Other large houses, all in this pseudo-French style, some with mansards and some without, in the Lake View district were those of Frank W. Palmer, W. C. Goudy, and J. A. Hack, the last house burned in the Fire; and in Kenwood the home of the Hon. N. B. Judd, friend of Lincoln and Minister to Berlin. Many others were built along the lines of the high-ceilinged, narrow-windowed house with moldings and ornaments which, though inspired by European models, were still a far, far cry away.

Carter Harrison in Caroline Kirkland's book, *When Chicago Was Young,* tells most entertainingly of the Kentucky colony on Ashland Avenue. The old Harrison homestead stood on the southwest corner of Jackson and Ashland, in those days called Reuben Street. He tells of the big "yards," the horses, cows and chickens everybody kept, and then of some of his father's neighbors before the Fire. The earliest of the settlers was Henry H. Honoré (the father of Mrs. Potter Palmer I), who died in 1916 at the age of ninety-two. His mansion with its "jutting bay windows, its spacious pillared front porch, its cupola and its cheery smiling grounds," stood at the southwest corner of Ashland and Jackson. Others he mentions, most of whom had fine houses in the neighborhood, were Judges J. S. Rogers, Samuel M. Moore and Murray F. Tuley. On the southwest corner of Madison and Ashland lived John E. Owsley. A. C. Badger, whose beautiful daughters were the pride of the town, lived at the southwest corner of

[11] Chamberlain, *op. cit.,* p. 349.

Ashland and Congress (Tyler in those days). Henry Waller lived at the northeast corner of Jackson and Ashland. And at the northeast corner of Van Buren stood the only house remaining today, that of Jasper D. Ward, congressman from his district.

Another house on the West Side notable in its day, was built by Peter Schuttler, who made a fortune out of manufacturing army carts during the Civil War. This huge place stood at Aberdeen and Adams and was erected in 1863. It varied from the usual formula with its high gables with a Gothic touch, but it had the great cupola over the entrance and the high narrow porch. We are told that the marble mantels were all carved in Italy.

On the near North Side, dominating the domestic scene, was the house of William B. Ogden, but it belongs to the Greek Revival category. It is difficult in the absence of pictorial illustration to determine the appearance of these pre-Fire houses, particularly when contemporaries describe them in terms of the pretty girls who lived there or of the wonderful biscuits the cook made.

Van Osdel had been the monarch of all he surveyed from the time he opened an architectural office in 1844 until the late fifties when inevitably other architects appeared upon the scene. One wonders that they didn't arrive sooner. With the revolution in style and taste that overthrew the Greek Revival, Van Osdel by no means hung up his T-square and put away his pencils in favor of the younger generation. In fact, some of his best buildings were erected after the Fire. Let us leave him a minute and mention some of his pre-Fire contemporaries.

His first and, for a while, only competitor was Edward Burling. Here was an architect who had a native promise of greatness. How tragic therefore his lack of preparation. He was born in Newburg, New York, in 1819. After a rudimentary schooling, he was apprenticed to a carpenter at the age of fourteen. He followed this trade until he came to Chicago in 1843, when he became a contractor and builder. His first taste of architecture was as superintendent on the old Tremont House. Next he represented William B. Ogden in his building interests and superintended the building of the famous Marine Hospital, a Greek Revival structure that looms up behind the second Fort Dearborn in so many of the old prints. Then he opened an office, "having an inborn taste for architecture," and his first product was one of the most delightful buildings produced in the Greek style. This was the house of Eli B. Williams, better known in after days as the Maison d'Orée, a fashionable tea-house on the southeast corner of Monroe and Wabash. Its portico of six Doric columns lives still in a rare photograph in the Burnham Library of the Art Institute. Burling's preparation, or lack of it, in the most technical of the arts is typical of the architects in the decade or more on each side of the Chicago Fire. They were for the most part builders attracted by the fame of the growing city, who came here as young men and climbed up from the carpenter's bench to the draughting-table.

Of all the buildings erected after the passing of the Greek Revival and before the Fire, the most meritorious, it seems to this chronicler, was the Chamber of Commerce which stood on the southeast corner of Washington and La Salle. This structure was designed by Burling and was completed in 1865. It measured ninety-three feet on Washington and one hundred eighty feet on La Salle, and was about one hundred feet in height. The façade was divided into three stories—a basement, a first story, a vast second story or *piano nobile,* as the Italians of the Renaissance would have called it, and a mansard roof.

THE ELI B. WILLIAMS HOUSE, KNOWN LATER AS THE "MAISON D'ORÉE"

Formerly on Wabash Avenue

THE CHAMBER OF COMMERCE

Built on the corner of Washington and LaSalle in 1865, the site of the First Baptist Church

This second story housed the Board of Trade in practically one majestic room one hundred forty-three feet long, eighty-seven feet wide, and forty-five feet high. We are told that the walls and ceiling were adorned with frescoes illustrative of the various industries and were illuminated by gas suspended on ten huge reflectors; also, that the building was heated by steam and cost, with the land, nearly a half million dollars. The exceedingly vigorous though restrained design in the contemporary French fashion was rather damned with faint praise by the critics of the time. Apparently this was because it was not overloaded with ornament and the architectural bombast and fussiness regarded in the sixties as fashionable. Andreas apologizes by saying,[12] "The design was not strictly in accordance with any known style of architecture, the aesthetic element in art being kept in subservience to the practical uses for which the building was planned and restricted by the economical limitations to the cost of the proposed structure."

St. James' Episcopal Church, standing today at the southeast corner of Cass (Wabash Avenue) and Huron Street, is another of Burling's works. The main body of the church was built in 1857, the excellent tower and west façade were added in 1868, and the building was entirely completed only some ten months before it was destroyed in the holocaust of '71. Two features redolent with heart interest remain today: the east side of the tower where the Fire King gnawed off the surface without breaking the bone, and the War Memorial in the north end of the vestibule. This memorial was designed by a firm of New York architects and is a well nigh perfect example of the Italianized Victorian Gothic of the late sixties, then

[12] Andreas, *op. cit.*, II, 358.

just imported. The fallen church shielded it with its body and it came unscathed through the fire.

Both the Tribune Building (1868) at the southeast corner of Dearborn and Madison, and the First National Bank on the southwest corner of State and Washington, also in the sixties, are by Burling. They are similar in design and identical in style, being in what the architects of the time regarded as Italian Renaissance. They share in part the restraint of the Chamber of Commerce and like it attain vigor by heavily rusticated piers and by a vigorously designed cornice.

After the Fire and until 1879 Burling formed a partnership with Dankmar Adler (later to become the partner of Louis Sullivan), and the two built and rebuilt a great many edifices. But we must not forget that we are now referring to Burling only in his pre-Fire aspect. Although we will hear of him again, we can leave him for a while, fully confident that he was "by nature generous and few stand higher in the list of Chicago's prominent, charitable, high-minded and upright citizens." [13]

More famous even than Burling was W. W. Boyington. Boyington came to Chicago in 1853 from Massachusetts. We are told that he received his "professional education" in great part from Professor Stone of New York City, who was a scientific as well as a practical architect. In order to get a practical knowledge of building with architecture as the goal, he entered a contractor's office and became himself a builder. His first commission in Chicago was the Central Union Depot. He early specialized in church building with St. Paul's, First Presbyterian, Wabash Avenue Methodist, First Baptist, North Presbyterian, Centenary, Ada Street Methodist, etc. Of our hotels, he designed the Grand Pacific, Sherman House, Massasoit

[13] *Industrial Chicago*, p. 596.

House and the Metropolitan. His public buildings included Dearborn Observatory and the University of
Chicago (adjoining Camp Douglas on Cottage Grove
Avenue and Thirty-fourth Street), and his railroad
stations are impressive, comprising work for the Lake
Shore and Michigan Southern and the Grand Union
Depot. And there were besides Crosby's Opera House,
Farwell Hall, Masonic Hall, etc. All of these are gone
with the Fire with one exception, and that is the loved
tower of the Chicago Water Works. This popular practitioner did his share of commercial buildings as well,
what with "marble front" blocks for the McCormicks
and Farwells and "marble blocks" on Lake Street. As
with Burling, regardless of the interruptions, we will have
to continue his career with the rebuilding of Chicago.

Of the building boom in full force at the time of the
Fire, Andreas comments: ". . . . building in Chicago was
progressing rapidly when the great disaster of 1871 fell
upon the city. Substantial brick, stone and iron-front
buildings were being erected with wonderful rapidity. On
State Street alone, during 1869-70, over forty stone buildings, all six stories high were constructed. . . . . The
eagerness to build pervading all classes of capitalists had
become almost a mania, the feverish excitement having
reached a point where it was no longer controlled by the
cooler judgment of the builders. Utility, speed of construction, and a prospective large return on the capital
invested, were the fundamental considerations."

Perhaps this haste explains, if it does not excuse, Boyington and his contemporaries for the character of work
which they consummated in the decade preceding the
Fire. Boyington's early work, except his churches, was
in the heavy-handed French mansard roof manner. The
Victorian Gothic revival only became manifest in the late

sixties. However, with all his faults we respect him for the Water Tower.

In the proud days before the Great War, when our Classic skyscrapers were rising up on every hand and Mr. Burnham was dangling the glories of his Chicago Plan before our eyes, with what disdain we regarded the old Water Tower which impinged so inconveniently on Michigan Avenue at Pearson Street. It was a symbol for all that was ugly and utterly old-fashioned in the "Mid-Victorian Age." It was called "goldfish bowl architecture" and was only tolerated because it was popularly thought to be the sole building in Chicago that survived the Fire. How much we misjudged our regard for Chicago's public relic number one was demonstrated when it was proposed to destroy it in order to allow the straightening of Michigan avenue. The howl of protest that went up must have astonished the city planners (who had only just before heard it derided) and delighted the shade of its author. Now it is proposed to make it the Palladium of the city with an eternal fire burning on its brow. So be it! It is not undeserving of the high honor.

The Water Tower is of course an adjunct of the old pumping-station, although between them now flows the plunging tide of Chicago traffic. The two were built on the site of the older pumping-station which occupied the plot of land fronting on Pine and bounded by Pearson street, Chicago Avenue and the Lake. According to Andreas, the "beautiful Water Tower" was completed in the early part of 1869. The building is described as "castellated Gothic with heavy battlemented corners, executed with solid rock face ashlar stone and cut stone trimmings, all the details being of a massive and permanent character." The tower, we are told, rises one hundred fifty-four feet to the top of the stone-work, above which extends the iron cupola. The tower, before these days of rest and honor, was an indispensable adjunct in the city's water supply, for it contained a 36 inch pipe of wrought iron 138 feet high. On its corner-stone is a bronze tablet that bears the inscription, "Laid by the Masonic Fraternity March 23, 1867."

Some of the buildings put up by Boyington before the Fire are: [14] 1853, Central Union Station; 1857, Universalist Church and St. Paul's (southwest corner Wabash and Van Buren); 1857, old University of Chicago, Cottage Grove and Thirty-fifth Street; Jones Hall (dedicated in 1859); 1865, Douglas Hall. Incidentally, the trustees had called for "a style of architecture purely Norman," which apparently meant early English Gothic; 1863, University of Chicago Observatory, given by Scammon; 1864, Democratic National Convention Hall, a circular building two hundred feet in diameter; 1863, Rosehill Cemetery Gate—Daniel H. Burnham told me, when a draughtsman in his office, to study it as an example of "crisp design," and I have venerated it ever since; 1866, McCormick Building, foot of Lake Street; 1865, Crosby's Opera House; 1866, Lake Shore and Michigan Southern Railroad Depot; 1869, Sherman House, and in the same year the Water Tower. With this start no wonder Boyington became the principal rebuilder of Chicago.

I have said before that the Fire was an episode rather than a turning-point in the development of Chicago architecture; yet there was a change, though a subtle one. About 1869, a boom year in construction, buildings were rapidly becoming more ornate. Before that time the typical office or commercial building above its very high cast-iron first story had a shaft of fairly plain wall four or five stories in height with windows crowned with ornamental

[14] H. Steward Leonard—Research.

lintels which might be square, segmental or arched. The whole building was then capped with a heavy bracketed cornice, often galvanized iron, and a flat roof. Two or three years before the Fire these buildings began very rapidly to get more elaborate. Perhaps it was the influence of the cast-iron fronts, such as the "Old Iron Block" built in 1856; perhaps it was a rapidly accumulating knowledge of European architecture; but more likely it was the élan that came from the responsibility and pride of being the builders of the wonder city of the world—exactly the same sentiment that animated the builders of Rome's *fora* and peristyles in the First Century. At the time of the Fire the Grand Pacific, Tremont and Sherman House had recently been completed, and the Nixon Building and Palmer House were almost ready to receive their roofs. Each of these was an exponent of the more abundant life in architecture; each expressed the confidence, energy and pride of Chicago, city of the West.

Although the names of Van Osdel, Burling and Boyington tower highest of pre-Fire architects, there were many others, of course, that helped build the lusty city that went down before the flames. It is impractical to write their biographies, but their names ought at least to be spread upon the record. There was Asher Carter, whose name first appears in the directory of 1849. He superintended the building of the Second Presbyterian Church, southwest corner of Wabash and Washington.

There was August Bauer, a German, who had worked on the Crystal Palace in New York as assistant architect and engineer.[15] He came to Chicago in 1853. Bauer built in 1868 a commercial structure, banking and office "house," at the southwest corner of Lake and La Salle for Charles F. Grey. It was faced with Athens marble, and

[15] Andreas *op. cit.*, II, 565.

described as "being of the Italian style of the Palladian School." He designed about the same time a building for the Commercial Insurance Company on Washington between Wells and La Salle, which is said to have been "built in the rich Italian style of the Venetian School," the front of white Athens marble "embellished with firemen's embellishments and other appropriate ornaments." It had fireproof vaults in the basement, first and second stories, spacious halls and elegant stairways. The entire structure was heated by the most approved system of low pressure steam. The inside was finished in various kinds of hardwood, among which black walnut and ash were the most prominent.

Another German-born architect was Otto H. Matz, born in 1830. He appears first in Chicago as architect for the Illinois Central Railroad and as such designed the terminal station at the foot of South Water street including the freight houses and shop, one of which, of Joliet limestone, remains south of the river at the foot of Wacker Drive. It and its neighbor to the east, the Sturges elevator, are the lone survivors of the Fire in the downtown district. After a Civil War career as engineer for General Grant, particularly in the Vicksburg campaign, he returned to Chicago, where he was made architect for the Board of Education. At the time of the Fire, he had nearly completed the Nixon Building, which survived the blast in large part. After the Fire he built the Alexian Brothers' Hospital and the Chicago Hospital for Women and Children, numerous business blocks and penthouses and the Criminal Court Building. His son, Herman Matz, has been prominent in the building industry for many years.

Another familiar name in the architecture of our city is Wheelock. The elder Wheelock was born in 1816 and came to Chicago in 1839. He worked on the Tremont

Hotel then being erected, but becoming disgusted with Chicago went back to New York, abandoning a half-acre of land that he had purchased at the corner of Wabash and Adams. After working with Minard Lefèvre, author of builders' handbooks, he returned to Chicago in 1856. With Boyington he designed in 1857 the old University of Chicago on Cottage Grove and Rhodes, which continued until 1886, when the buildings were taken down and the material sold. He also designed with Boyington, the Baptist Theological Seminary on Rhodes Avenue. This major work was accomplished after the Fire.

Ten years ago the white beard, the silver mane and the bright eyes of Edward Baumann were familiar and welcome sights at every meeting of the Illinois Chapter of the American Institute of Architects. He was over ninety at that time, having been born near Danzig in 1838. I remember his telling me that his father had been a soldier of Frederick the Great. He arrived in Chicago in 1857 and for a time was associated with Burling. Baumann's fame rests on his authorship of a pamphlet on foundations [16] published shortly after the Fire, which had a profound influence on the construction of Chicago's subsequent buildings and must therefore be discussed a bit later. In those days it seemed the rule for architects to shift or trade partners with facility, and we find Baumann in 1852 as partner with Burling until three years later, when he joined forces with Van Osdel. After a hiatus of seven years, in which he regained his health and built himself up as a contractor, we find him again an architect with a cousin, Edward Baumann, as his partner—and that brings us to the Fire with his principal service still to be told.

[16] "The Art of Preparing Foundations for all kinds of Buildings with Illustrations of the Method of Isolated Piers as followed in Chicago"—Published by J. M. Wing, Chicago, 1873.

William Thomas descended from a line of architects. He arrived in Chicago in 1856. With his son, C. P. Thomas, as a partner, he specialized in residences. They constructed many post-Fire houses along East Ontario and Ohio with an English touch of excellent taste and varied material. Cord H. Gottig from Germany came in 1857. He became the architect of the Illinois Central Railway. Willoughby J. Edbrook was born in Chicago of English parents, and began practice in 1867. John C. Cochrane came in 1855 and again in 1864. He specialized in churches and residences. George O. Garnsey was the architect of the State House at Springfield and specialized in public buildings throughout the state.

Industrial Chicago states that T. V. Wadskier was a Dane, but Richard E. Schmidt who knew him says that he was an Englishman, born in St. Croix in the West Indies in 1827, and that he came to Chicago in 1857. He had a fashionable clientèle and built, among others, the J. W. Doane house (destroyed), next north to Marshall Field's, recently the Bauhaus on Prairie. As good an epitome of Chicago's architects as any is found in an article in the *Tribune,* written apparently in the spring of 1873. The caption is characteristic—"Chicago Architects, the men who have made our city the handsomest and safest in the world. Europeans may now come here to study correct architecture." These are the men listed as the "first architects" of the post-Fire city:

J. M. Van Osdel

"He came to Chicago in 1837. Think of the changes he has witnessed since then! With an energy which has known no abatement he works on as blithely as hitherto, and it is to be hoped that he will continue for many years to come."

W. W. Boyington

"He gives more attention to the planning and construction of first class and large hotels than any other architect in this country."

E. Burling

(He gets the most space.) "The leading characteristics of the buildings erected under his professional care are solidity and thoroughness of construction, elegance and simplicity of design, the avoidance of frippery and unnecessary or vulgar ornamentation, and above all things, adaptation to the purposes for which they are to be used."

C. P. Thomas

"His works since the Fire are equalled by few in beauty of design and boldness and elegance of detail."

Bauer

"Among our best educated and most experienced architects, the name of Mr. Augustus Bauer is conspicuous."

A. L. Wheelock

"One of the most distinguished and successful architects, who has designed some of the finest structures in this city devoted to business and to public and private uses."

Otto H. Matz

"In the great competition for the Court House, Mr. Matz was awarded the first prize of $5,000, and it still remains a riddle to the tax-payers why this plan is now completely ignored."

A. J. Smith

"This gentleman has contributed largely to the architecture of the city, having built some of the finest bank, college and commercial buildings here."

F. B. Hamilton

"He has practised his profession during the past ten years and many of our largest and most elegant public and private buildings are products of his skill and taste.

C. M. Palmer

"Office entresol Palmer House, is very prominent in his profession.

Cass Chapman

"Has made a special study of Church architecture."

Furst and Flanders

"Rising and reliable young architects."

THE CHICAGO FIRE

October 8-10, 1871

Although the Great Fire destroyed goods and chattels, intangible property and human lives, and though the principal substance of the holocaust was buildings, nevertheless, what captivated the attention of the world and still fires the imagination as perhaps no other conflagration has ever done is a chapter in drama, not in architecture. From the unproved incident of the cow kicking over the kerosene lamp in Mrs. O'Leary's barn to the citizens who on the North Side buried their children in the sand and waded into Lake Michigan up to their necks, the appeal is that of intense personal interest. Much talk there was then of the destruction of irreplaceable architectural masterpieces. Yet the argument that the Chicago Fire revolutionized the art or even the science of building in Chicago or in other local cities could hardly be proved. One might have hoped that in the white heat of such a blast the slag of our artistic impurities would be skimmed off, or that the phoenix, arising from the embers, would look more like an eagle and less like a turkey buzzard; but that was not the case. A greater effort was made to fireproof buildings, and some larger buildings were built, as will be brought out, but the Fire was no ending of an epoch nor a turning-point in the road. Nevertheless, it cannot be ignored and the mere cataloguing of its achievements fills with respect and awe the mind of today.

The axis of the fire was a line in a north-northeasterly direction from the corner of DeKoven and Jefferson Streets to the Water Tower on Chicago Avenue. This line passes through the Court House and City Hall. On either side of it the fire spread—on the North to a little beyond Fullerton Avenue and on the South Side to Congress Street. Within these limits it made a clean sweep of practically everything between the north and south branches of the river and the lake, except that on the North Side it did not spread west of Halsted Street. On the West Side the area consumed comprised one hundred ninety-four acres.[17] On the South Side four hundred sixty acres were burned, and on the North, fourteen hundred seventy. This comprised on the West Side five hundred buildings, mostly inferior, three thousand six hundred fifty on the South Side, mostly business, and thirteen thousand three hundred, mostly residential, on the North Side. This totalled nearly three and a third square miles. One hundred thousand people were rendered homeless. Some of the estimates of building losses are interesting, such as: eighty business blocks, $8,515,000; railroad depots, warehouses and Chamber of Commerce, $2,700,000; hotels $3,100,000; theaters, etc., $865,000; daily news-

---

[17] Andreas *op. cit.*, II, 760. A map of the "burned district" published at the time by R. P. Studley Company shows the fire on the West Side extending west to Halsted and south to Canalport Avenue about twice the area mentioned above.

papers, $888,000; one hundred other business buildings, $1,008,420; churches, $2,989,000; public schools, $249,780; other buildings and public improvements, $32,764,800— making a total of $53,080,000.[18] Losses of produce, business goods, personal effects, allowing a $10,000,000 salvage in foundation and building material, made a grand total loss of $186,000,000. Of the wealth of the city, one-third was destroyed by the fire. Ninety thousand persons were rendered homeless and about three hundred lost their lives. The report of the Board of Public Works in 1871 gives us the further information that the fire burned with wonderful rapidity, consuming on an average sixty-five acres per hour, and destroying on an average $125,000 per minute. In the vast amount of eye-witness stories, all agree that the conflagration was almost completely smokeless. In consequence the awful magnificence of the spectacle could have been seldom equalled in human experience.

In the second ward there was a large proportion of wooden buildings giving way towards the north to stone and brick. Here stood the grandiose Palmer Hotel, opened in March, 1871, and the tragic Bigelow House with its roses on the tables awaiting the grand opening. The Grand Pacific, also hardly completed, magnificent and costly, stood proudly on LaSalle and Jackson. Some of the railway terminals were in the second ward, including the Rock Island and the Michigan Southern. The twentieth ward north of the river was more combustible. For three or more blocks there were private houses, many of stone; on Kinzie street there was a great market; while for miles to the north stretched buildings generally of wood. Along the north side of the river were the McCormick Reaper works, two elevators and freight depots. The ward con-

[18] *Ibid.* II, 760. Contents of churches and public schools only included.

tained many of the famous churches, such as St. James'
Episcopal; Unity, Robert Collyer's church, as it was
usually called; and the New England Church on Washington Square. Among the Catholics were the Cathedral
of the Holy Name, St. Joseph's Church (German) and
the Orphan Asylum. There were two hospitals, one stone
public school of the modern style and four brick schools.
Towards the east near the lake were the famous water
works and several large breweries, and also the supposedly
fireproof buildings of the Historical Society and Rush
Medical College. The chronicler made the further interesting observation that the population of the north division
was mostly of foreign birth, the sixteenth and seventeenth
wards being predominantly German, the eighteenth, Irish,
and the nineteenth and twentieth, mixed.

An old gentleman told me that the greatest thrill in
his long and varied life was experienced on that lurid day
of October 11, 1871. The fire, having leaped the river, had
begun to devour the North Side. His father, giving up the
last vestige of hope of saving the big house, gathered the
family with the choicest of their possessions in the front
yard. As they were bidding adieu to the old homestead
my friend, a boy of fourteen, suddenly remembered that
he had left the most treasured of his possessions, a new
shot-gun, in his bedroom closet. Slipping away from the
retreating family, he ran into the house and, three steps
at a time, up to his bedroom in the third story. There
was his gun and also a box of cartridges on the closet shelf.
He mechanically loaded each barrel and slowly descended
the long walnut stairway now glowing in the flames practically at the back door. With his gun under his arm he
walked into the front parlor for a last look. For as long
as he could remember he had scarcely been allowed to
enter, let alone play, in this awesome and sacred place

with its marble mantel, its glass case full of curios and particularly its two huge French mirrors with their carved gilt frames, which reached from floor to ceiling at each end of the room. These, its cachet of elegance, were the family's greatest pride and responsibility. And now he stood in the center of this holy of holies, his long, long thoughts strangely disturbed by the muffled roar of the approaching holocaust and the dancing reflections in the great mirrors. Slowly he cocked both barrels, raised the gun to his shoulder, aimed it at the center of mirror number one, bang! and twenty-five hundred dollars went into a thousand tinkling pieces. With the coolness that characterizes all big game hunters, he turned about, took careful aim and bang! mirror number two bit the dust and littered the Brussels carpet. He then tucked his faithful gun under his arm, blithely ran out of the door and up Cass Street to join his fleeing elders who were all unaware of what a wonderful world it was.

The exciting experiences of our citizenry, tragic and humorous as well, the spontaneous and genuine aid from the other cities of the commonwealth, the tremendous interest awakened in foreign lands by the tragedy—excellent reading as they are—must all make way here for observations relative to building materials and fire hazards. Van Osdel, you will remember, in his comments on Chicago architecture blamed balloon construction in large degree for the extent of the fire and the speed of its progress. Certainly the set-up for a dangerous conflagration was about perfect and Chicago realized it. Here was a large city built in great part of combustible materials, situated on a flat plain, exposed to high winds prevalent at all seasons, but particularly to hot southwest winds blowing from the direction where fire hazard was the greatest, a poor district of wooden buildings, lumber and coal yards, and light manufacturing. All that was needed was a dry season, a strong southwest wind and a kindling blaze in the southwest corner. This situation occurred in exaggerated degree October 8, 1871. The season was unprecedented for its droughts, the wind was a gale, and the O'Leary barn on DeKoven Street was in exactly the right spot. Furthermore, the Fire King had drawn a high trump in the exhaustion of the fire department, which had been continuously fighting fires for a week or more, particularly the severe one that threatened the city on October 7 and burned four blocks between Van Buren and Adams and Clinton and the river.

Fire limits had long been established within which no building with a frame exterior might be built. This did not prevent the erection of wooden interiors and tar roofs on buildings whose exterior walls were of masonry. The fire limits in 1871,[19] generally speaking, extended from Twenty-Second Street on the south to Illinois Street on the north with a further projection of both sides of Wells Street as far as Chicago Avenue. West of the river there was an irregular area from Van Buren to Lake and west to Clinton and Halsted. The ordinances were poorly enforced, however, and no effort was made to tear down existing wooden buildings. In fact, it was stated in the *Tribune* editorial that half the buildings within the fire limits were of wood.

William B. Ogden with his usual clear vision perceived the futility of even "fireproof" buildings in such a blast, for he writes: "The reason that buildings, men or anything did not withstand the torrents of the fire is explained by the fact that the fire was accompanied by the fiercest tornado of wind ever known to blow here, and it acted like a perfect blow pipe driving the brilliant blaze hun-

[19]*Chicago Tribune* of October 9, 1872.

dreds of feet with so perfect a combustion that it consumed the smoke, and its heat was so great that fireproof
buildings sank before it almost as readily as wood." An
examination of the ruins, as depicted in countless photographs, shows the Government Post-Office and Customs
Building rising with its four walls mostly intact from the
utter destruction about it. As this building was the depository of vast sums for the purchase of government supplies,
in addition to housing the United States mails, every precaution had been taken to make it fireproof. It was
furthermore designed and inspected by government
architects and doubtless was honestly built. It will serve,
therefore, as the best type of the fireproof building of its
day and as a typical example of the resistance, or rather
lack of it, of such a building to the conflagration.

The edifice stood on the northwest corner of Dearborn and Monroe, not far, therefore, from the axis of the
fire. It was eighty by one hundred fifty feet, three stories
and basement in height, and cost $365,000. The construc-
tion, which particularly interests us, was, according to
Henry H. Nash, cashier of the U. S. Depository, as follows: [20] It was built of Lemont stone backed with brick,
very substantial and designed to be fireproof. The floors
were supported by cast-iron columns. These supported
"hollow iron," which means cast-iron girders about six by
eighteen inches, and between them wrought-iron "I"
beams, eight inches deep and about three feet apart.
Between the beams sprang brick arches, filled in on top
to a level surface, on which rested the finished wood
floor. All the exterior windows appear to have been pro-
vided originally with iron shutters. Given the fire, two
other causes contributed to the complete destruction of
the interior of this building together with its contents.

---

[20] Narrative of Henry H. Nash in Andreas, *op. cit.*, II, 721.

The first was the iron shutters, probably on the west and north walls only,[21] those on the first story having been removed the year before. Nash, who was present, says that the iron shutters above were all closed in time and that the fire entered through the exposed first story windows on the west side. The second was the supporting cast-iron columns. These were undoubtedly uncovered. In fact, the great lesson of the fire, largely drawn from the example of this building, was the necessity of protecting all structural iron work with a covering of fire clay, tile, terra cotta or brick. Cast iron melts at the comparatively low temperature of 2741 degrees, and the temperatures created by the conflagration were estimated to reach the height of more than 3000 degrees. It could have been but a few minutes before the columns collapsed and probably the iron girders as well, which were also unprotected. This catastrophe let down the entire interior of the building into the basement. It was the fabulous contents of the vaults and their fate, however, that intrigued the populace. The government funds were locked in a vault constructed of three inches of boiler plate and "chilled" cast iron and walled up with brick. The whole unfortunately rested on the above described treacherous cast-iron columns and beams and in consequence the entire treasure chest was precipitated into the basement. In its violent descent one corner split open, and, when four days later the smoking mass had cooled off, it was found that $1,034,000 had gone up literally in smoke and that $435,000, mostly in gold and silver, could be salvaged by cleaning or reminting, as a great part of it was a conglomeration of melted gold, silver and nickel. Panora-

---

[21] A photograph shows shutters on the interior of the east and west walls, a very unusual arrangement.

mas [22] and other depictions of the holocaust tell the same melancholy story—the complete destruction of all interiors and for the most part of the exteriors as well, though here and there rise the gaunt faces with their sightless eyes of many a noble structure. The scarred walls of the Grand Pacific Hotel, the Court House, the First National Bank, the Potter Palmer Building, the Honoré Building, the Second Presbyterian Church, like horrid fangs, project from the toothless city, while the skeletons of trees and the deserted wastes bring back visions of a No Man's Land in a World War.

> "On three score spires had sunset shone,
> Where ghostly sunrise looked on none;
> Men clasped each other's hands and said:
> The City of the West is dead."

What the name Jenney means to skeleton construction, Johnson means to fireproofing in Chicago. George H. Johnson was an Englishman, born in 1830, who came to America in 1852 and to Chicago in 1860. He associated himself with Van Osdel. Johnson had been manager of the Architectural Iron Works in New York City, and brought with him the new and fashionable custom of building façades of cast iron. Van Osdel was converted to the idea, and together they built four iron-front buildings, all of large size, on Lake Street. Elaboration in iron is much easier than in stone, as one mold suffices in countless repetitions as contrasted with individual hand-carving for each and every part. It is fair to say, then, that in an age when elaboration was the goal, the be-columned and be-corniced façades of cast iron made a profound impression and were unquestionably largely responsible for the elaboration of the stone façade, the

[22] Andreas *op. cit.*, Vol. I, opposite page 758.

superimposed orders, the encircling cornices, the moldings and the keystones that characterized the buildings
immediately before and for five or six years after the Fire.
We have, then, the ridiculous situation of stone imitating
cast iron which was imitating stone!

Johnson, though his fame rests on fireproofing, is entitled to further laurels for his all-unconscious influence
in the aesthetics of the office buildings of his time. He was
in New York when the big news of the Fire was flashed
around the world. He hastened back to Chicago. All of
his studies and cogitations of fireproofing seem to have
been suddenly jelled in the presence of what had been
Chicago smouldering at his feet, a mass of calcined stone,
melted iron and broken bricks—all materials that man
had fondly believed to be fireproof. The vision that he
saw was a hollow, hard-burned tile of fire clay which
could be made in almost any desired form suitable for
covering iron columns and beams, forming the floor by
means of arch construction between the beams for the
constructing of partitions and for backing up exterior walls.

On the southwest corner of Dearborn and Washington
there is an old timer, with several added stories and the
faded name of "Equitable" on its brow. This was originally the Kendall Building. In 1873 Mr. Johnson and a
number of gentlemen prominent in the building interests
and in civic affairs saw erected the first hollow tile fireproofing in the modern world, and the inauguration of the
system of fireproof construction that became universal up
to the invention of re-enforced concrete. I won't go so far
as to say that this veteran should be preserved as an
historic monument, but at least someone should pin a
badge on his worn lapel, stating his distinguished services
to mankind.

A huge two-volume book, *Industrial Chicago—The*

Building Interests, ranks next to old reliable Andreas as a means of solving some of the mysteries that surrounded the architectural aspirations of Chicago in the twenty years of which the Fire was the pivot. There is a long chapter entitled "Chicago Architectural Styles." Along with a vast amount of statistical information is merged a vast ignorance of architecture either as art or history. For instance: ". . . . the Doric and Ionic temples [referring to the Greek Revival] erected here in the forties . . . . were not duplicated. They made way for the Romanesque-Byzantine and for that Gothic which could lose itself in the air or merge into immensity rather than crawl in the old marsh." [23] However, in the next paragraph the author says more accurately, referring to the beauty and utility of the French Renaissance, "Chicago realized this in the fifties, and when her early architects were asked to revel in beauty, they selected one or other of the styles peculiar to the Italian or French Schools." In a paragraph farther on he confirms some of our surmises. He says, ". . . . From 1849 to the summer of 1865 comparative advances in the building arts were evident. Prospective builders talked with architects and were shown illustrations of façades by every originator of styles." He mentions as epochal buildings of this period the Old Board of Trade, the Court House and the Tremont House. "Brick was fast displacing wood; house-moving became a distinct trade; frame dwellings were moved to the outskirts of the city, and in their place rose up solid blocks of brick business houses. It was an extraordinary building epoch, when the time and place are considered; but architecture scarcely entered into the calculations of owners. It was the astylar age of Chicago, materialistic to a degree, severely plain if not actually primitive." His

[23] *Industrial Chicago—The Building Interests,* I, 53.

references to house-moving not only explain in part the rapid disappearance of the Greek Revival house, but stir the pages of memory. Who of us who knew the eighties and the early nineties can forget the peripatetic house-moving in microscopic stages through our quiet streets; the excitement of the house owners over their threatened elms; the great horse that patiently tugged around and around the windlass to the fascinating sound of creaking chains and squeaking rollers, whilst the old house, temporarily shorn of its verandas and chimneys, crept up on his heels? He ascribes Boyington's design for Crosby's Opera House, built in 1865, as our first envoy into the field of sophisticated architecture. Incidentally, he describes it as of the Norman-Romanesque-Byzantine style with Italian ornament and a mansard roof.

Perhaps a direct way to get at the Fire-change of architecture would be to compare a building erected shortly before the Fire with its successor which rose immediately from its ashes. Such a building was the Honoré, standing now on the northwest corner of Adams and Dearborn. Before the Fire it had five stories, the first of cast iron raised several steps above the sidewalk. A basement was reached by steps down from the sidewalk. The four stories above the first were plain except for thin rusticated piers that separated the façade into wide bays, and an equally timid band course at the third floor. A very heavy and coarse cornice with huge brackets capped the whole. The general effect is of a barbarous building built by an architect who was evidently guessing at some foreign buildings which he hoped to emulate.

The new Honoré Building, on the same site as the old, is symbolic of the vivid style with which the architects of Chicago's resurrection wished to clothe her apotheosis. The building is six stories high and of impressive dimen-

Burke and Koretke photograph from Joseph T. Ryerson Collection

THE COURT HOUSE BEFORE THE FIRE

Showing successive additions to Van Osdel's second structure of 1853. The alarm bell sounded from the dome

THE HONORÉ BUILDING, ADAMS AND DEARBORN

Before the fire

sion, being one hundred fourteen feet on Adams and one hundred ninety on Dearborn. Each story is separated from its neighbor by a cornice supported by columns one story in height. Completely filling the space between the columns is a deeply recessed arched window with its arches resting on capped piers. The whole is crowned by a rich, bracketed cornice. This is the most sumptuous architectural arrangement known in Classic architecture and was greatly favored by the Venetian architects of the Renaissance. It can be seen in the Libraria Vecchio and the Palazzo Grimoni in Venice. In fact, this last-named building by Sammichele is said to have been the inspiration of the Honoré façade. The architect was C. M. Palmer, the man who succeeded Van Osdel in the building of the Palmer House after the Fire. Of the few forlorn survivors in the Loop of these sumptuous façades that Chicago pointed to with pride in the ten years that followed the Fire, few, perhaps, have gone the limit with an architectural order for every story, but every one, almost without exception, has a cornice separating every floor, as, for instance, the corner building still standing at 36 West Randolph, or the one at 111 Clark. Perhaps we should give C. M. Palmer more credit in directing Chicago's post-Fire architecture than he usually gets. The chroniclers say little about him except that he was born in Michigan and began to practice in Chicago about 1866.

In a typically "booster" publication [24] in behalf of the "live real estate men" there was published a series of woodcuts on a large scale of the principal buildings erected in the first two years after the Fire. Of these very few stand today. Shabby and forlorn and, like old and poor dependents, a source of chagrin and worry to their owners,

[24] "The Land Owner. One Year After the Fire," 1873; "Greater Chicago," 1875; "Two Years After the Fire," 1874.

they were, however, eloquent of the architectural taste of
the time, and a few of them should be spread upon the
record: The American Express Company Building on
Monroe near State, five stories random stone-facing in
two shades, Eastlake in style with high mansard roof,
pinnacles, iron cresting and ornamental chimneys; the
Palmer House, southeast corner of State and Monroe,
running through then as now to Wabash avenue and
occupying nearly half the block. The building was the
pride of Chicago *resurgitans*. It was seven stories high
including the mansard roof. The publisher states under
the illustration, "The largest and most costly Hotel building—entirely fireproof." The façade was divided horizontally into three divisions. Each contained two stories with
two-story pilasters between the windows. All was stone
except the shop windows, which were of iron. The Bowen
Building, State and Madison, was similar in style to the
Palmer House, being four stories and attic in height. The
La Salle Block, La Salle and Madison, was five stories
high, French but *sans* mansard, for which was substituted
a huge iron cresting. The façade was divided by a cornice
at each floor and an order for each story. The Major
Block, La Salle and Madison, was very similar. It was
given over to the building interests, to judge from the
signs that were painted or carved all over its façade. The
Otis Block, La Salle and Madison, was plainer but not,
therefore, purer. It too was French. One had to mount
eleven exterior steps to reach the first floor. The Tremont
House, Lake and Dearborn Streets, was also obviously
based on the New Louvre, with mansard domes, pavilions,
etc. It was a huge building, six stories in height. The Portland Block, Washington and Dearborn, comes as a relief,
for its style is Gothic—the Ruskinized Gothic, with dark
and light stone bands so fashionable a year or so later.

Here one walked up thirteen outside stairs to reach the floor of the Third National Bank. The Windett Building, Randolph and State, and the Fullerton and King Blocks, Washington and Dearborn, repeat all the features and barbarisms of the La Salle Block, while a building at the northeast corner of Madison and Dearborn actually has a stone corner stairway fourteen steps high projecting out onto the sidewalk. The Honoré Block on Dearborn, the Honoré Hotel, Adams and Dearborn, Nixon Building, La Salle and Monroe, and the Lake Shore and Michigan Southern stations on Van Buren, head of La Salle, ring few changes on the florid French importation. The Hale Block, however, on the southeast corner of State and Washington, lends a piquant interest in its extraordinary forms, in which the architect apparently attempts to combine Gothic and Classic. Another example seems to be Book-Seller Row in State Street. Projecting columns, tortured cornices, wreaths and garlands hang upon its façade. The most interesting building is the Ballard Block, Wabash and Monroe. Were it not for its English basement, it would appear to be of a vintage thirty years later.

Perhaps, after all, it is futile to run to earth the designs of the post-Fire architects in the fashion that prevailed from 1870 to 1880. It certainly is beyond our province to blame them or to criticize them. Without technical training themselves, and in a time when the details and earmarks of the Styles were the *sine qua non* of elegance in a structure, it is hard to see how they could have done otherwise. It would seem that today when functionalism is in the saddle and ornament is taboo that an intelligent architect, well-grounded in the engineering and structural lore of his profession but without technical knowledge of its aesthetics or its architectural history, has a better chance to produce what would pass for good architecture than at any time in the last hundred years. Therefore our commiserations to Boyington, Burling, Baumann, etc., who had to occupy the center of the stage without knowing the lines.

France was the most popular of our sources of inspiration. The buildings of the time in France famous enough to reach Chicago by way of reproductions and photographs were the Pavillon Richelieu by Visconti, and the Pavillon de la Bibliothèque by Lefuel, both large additions to the Louvre. These gave us mansard roofs, huge dormer windows, free-standing columns, rustications, statuary. Most certainly the Palmer House was strongly influenced by the additions to the Louvre. Furthermore, Richard M. Hunt, who received the first American *diplomé* in architecture at the Beaux Arts, returned in 1855. Hunt was the most distinguished practitioner of his time and introduced contemporary French architecture to America. He also had worked on the extension of the Louvre. The next great edifice in its influence was the Library of Ste. Geneviève in Paris which was finished in 1852. Its architect was Labrouste. Its style was called *Néo-Grec,* corresponding in a sense to the Greek Revival in England and America. It came late, however, and its style was too sophisticated to influence greatly our architects.

It may be of interest, not so much in the matter of architecture as in honoring the energy and optimism of Chicago's citizens, to mention in order a few of the buildings erected immediately after the Fire. The distinction of being the very first, excepting Mr. Kerfoot's shanty raised on a hot and still smoking site, was the Henry Fuller building on River Street, which was a three-story brick and cost $18,000. Cyrus McCormick showed his confidence with six important edifices: northwest corner Lake and Michigan, five stories, $100,000; two stores on

Lake Street just west of Michigan, $60,000; southwest corner Randolph and Dearborn, $150,000; and the Reaper Block, Clark and Washington, $200,000. This structure is still standing, with a story or two added. We are told it was built with a mansard roof. It was designed by Van Osdel. The Drake family built on Wabash and Washington five stories at a cost of $150,000. The Couch family came to the front with a five-story building on Lake Street and two others on South Water at an aggregate cost of $150,000. The Hall and Ayers Block, Insurance Exchange, and the Oriental, were constructed, it is interesting to discover, from old plans, perhaps some of those that Van Osdel buried in a pit under the Palmer House.

Michigan Avenue was in those days, as in these, *sui generis*. There was a slumbering conviction that it ought to be the most beautiful street in the country, but some doubt as to how to bring this about. Since 1852, when the Illinois Central Railroad received permission from the Legislature to build a branch from the terminus at Twelfth Street to Fort Dearborn, the people had railroad tracks in their front yard. The only attempt at beautification was a long narrow strip of lawn between the street and the lake, edged with little trees and surrounded by a modern fence. The avenue at this time with its white-columned churches, its wooden houses with their wide lawns, its sheltering trees, looked very much indeed like a street in a New England town. At the time of the Fire the character or, more properly, the appearance of Michigan Avenue had changed greatly. Terrace Row, the fashionable abode of the wealthy, and eleven fine houses, filling the block to the south of it, were all of the modish French style with Athens marble fronts, verandas with iron trellises, cast-iron fences, etc. They were the last victims of the "fire fiend," as the conflagration was unkindly called.

All lovers of old Chicago are familiar with the wooden shanty erected by W. D. Kerfoot on Washington between Dearborn and Clark on October 10, 1871. It bore a sign "Kerfoot's Block" and the observation "All gone but wife, children and energy," a splendid challenge to the forces of discouragement. This was the first building erected after the Fire. However, within six weeks 318 permanent buildings had been started with a frontage of three and a half miles. The *Tribune* of October 25 makes the interesting comment that the buildings then under construction were, owing to the stress of circumstances, of an "excessively plain style," with fronts of red or white pressed brick with brick cornices, but it added that the architects were swamped with plans for elaborate structures to go ahead in the spring and that the present was no time to speculate on the appearance of Chicago when rebuilt.

Of the lesser luminaries who shone through the dying smoke of the Fire, none was more interesting than Adolph Cudell, who hailed from Aix La Chapelle, and came to Chicago immediately after the fire. The firm was known as Cudell and Blumenthal. Richard E. Schmidt began his distinguished architectural career in Cudell's office as a draughtsman. He describes him as a handsome man with black hair in Apollo-like ringlets, and as a draughtsman of ability with a meticulous technique. He introduced a great deal of Greek detail into his buildings, but Schmidt says he doesn't think they were inspired by the *Néo-Grec,* fashionable in Paris in the fifties, but by Greek architecture direct, and cites from his memory Stuart and Revett's *Antiquities of Athens* and Bötticher's *Tektonic der Hellenen,* etc., as having been in his library. Cudell later became a designer and manufacturer of fine cabinet work and furniture. It was said that many places of entertainment on the North Side took pride in the possession of various pieces from the hand of Cudell, obtained in his later years as payment in kind.

Aldine Square was a famous work by Cudell, as also was the Perry H. Smith house on Pine and Huron. He likewise built a row of houses on Indiana Avenue between Sixteenth and Eighteenth on the west side of the street, now destroyed. His *chef d'oeuvre,* however, was the Cyrus McCormick house still standing at 675 Rush Street. Aldine Square was in what is now in the center of the chocolate belt. It was rather obscurely located on Vincennes near Thirty-seventh. It occupied three sides of the little square, whose tiny empty lagoon and rickety rustic bridges later looked peculiarly desolate in a grassless waste. They must all have possessed a pristine loveliness and charm almost unique in a city where little attention was paid to landscape architecture except for canna and flower beds of the star and anchor variety. The buildings were continuous, save for two openings at the inner corners, and presented a carefully studied composition of two and three stories on a high English basement. Uniformity was attempted by a strong continuous cornice at the top of the second story, and variety was gained by strong semi-circular bays with flat domes, pediments and occasional third stories.

The material was Lemont stone (Athens marble) laid in vertical slabs with incised artificial joints. The style was of great interest. The cornices and moldings were vigorous and well drawn, the corners of lintels and jambs were chamfered, the ornament was both free-standing and incised. The stone columns had capitols of Greek Ionic ancestry, and all of the carvings and moldings had a crispness and snap that could have come from only one place, and that was Paris. As I see it, Aldine Square in style was a melange of the work of the distinguished Frenchmen of the time of Napoleon III—Hittorf, Labrouste, and Garnier all looked down at us from the façades of Aldine Square.

Far more famous than Aldine Square, in fact only second to Potter Palmer's castle on the Drive, was and is the Cyrus McCormick house on the west half of the square facing on Rush, between Huron and Erie. This house was begun in 1875 and completed in 1879. The interior was designed and installed by L. Marcott and Company of New York. This huge brown stone mansion proclaims to even a greater extent than Aldine Square its French ancestry. Here, however, the inspiration has been the new additions to the Louvre and the Paris Opera, rather than the *Néo-Grec*. The Louvre is announced by the high mansard roof with its elaborate cresting, its mansard cupola, its bull's-eye windows and its rusticated stone work done exactly after the fashion of, say, the Pavilion Richelieu, while the banded columns, the garlands, the richness of ornament, certainly stem from Charles Garnier's famous Nouvelle Opéra, the architectural wonder of the world in the reign of Napoleon III.

The Cyrus McCormick house brings up again the genesis of our architecture of the sixties and the seventies. It has many peculiarities, some of which may well be discussed in detail. For instance, a favorite device of the time was incising a design in line in the face of the stone. The line was usually about half to an inch in width and a half inch deep. It took the form either of a free design of scrolls or geometrical forms sometimes interlaced, or else an architectural form like a cornice or trim about a window or door. Sometimes it was used very sparingly and in connection with moldings and ornament cut in relief, as in the Cyrus McCormick house and in Aldine Square.

In the C. L. Larrabee house, 12 West Walton, by Otto Matz, architect, the stone window-heads set in the brick wall have quaint little floral scrolls deeply incised. This house was a favorite resort of Jane Addams, where she visited her friend Marie Rozet Smith. Sometimes, as in a building at 507 North Clark, a locality which preserves almost all of its post-Fire buildings intact, the incised lines are an adjunct to projecting cornices and capitals. A passer-by would think that all the architectural features of this rich façade, dated 1873, were in relief, whereas the arches (archivolts) and window trim are imitated by lines sunk into the stone. The ultimate is reached in the building at the southeast corner of State and Grand, or in a row of houses at 62 West Delaware, where all the architectural features except the main cornice are incised in line on a flat façade. There are a number of explanations of this curious but very popular fashion. In almost every case the façade is of Athens marble, large slabs four to six inches thick, set on edge. In a great many cases, these had false joints, and it was a simple step to extend the falsities around window and door with similar incisions.

The last of the Parvenu Mohicans in architecture was the Board of Trade Building, whose corner-stone was laid December 13, 1882. One wonders how W. W. Boyington, the architect, could have failed to sense the coming of a new conqueror in the architectural dominion.

Trinity Church, H. H. Richardson's epoch-making masterpiece, had been thrown open to the world at the beginning of 1877, and its influence with that of other buildings by Richardson had already changed almost entirely the architectural complexion of the country. Even without the Romanesque Revival, had Boyington never heard of the Free Classic, generally known as the Queen Anne, the wife, so to speak, of the Romanesque Revival? Together they were producing a tremendous family and Chicago was one of the favorite birthplaces.

There have been many other tragic incidents of architectural children born of aged parents who came into a world that didn't want them—Gothic churches unfinished at the coming of the Renaissance and before our eyes today; the Cathedral of St. John in New York, designed just before the 1893 World's Fair and so unfashionable in its Romanesque clothes that its style had to be changed before sufficient funds could be found to complete it.

At the time the corner-stone of the Board of Trade was laid, already in Chicago had been built, or plans completed for, the huge Montauk Block, the Portland Block, the Town of Pullman, the Chicago, Burlington and Quincy Depot and many others, all in the new Romanesque or allied style. Boyington designed a monstrous affair one hundred seventy-four feet on Jackson extending two hundred twenty-five feet south between Sherman and LaSalle. The building was one hundred feet high with a tower rising to two hundred twenty-five feet. One of the sensations of my youth was seeing the top of this tower taken down, for Mother Nature had made a bear raid in the building and the tower was sinking fast. The whole exterior of the building was constructed of granite except the tower of the lantern, which was of ornamental iron. The author of *Industrial Chicago* calls it in one place "Commercial Gothic" with "Italian Ornament" and in another "American Gothic." It, however, was a symphony of all architectural clichés of the early seventies—Eastlake ornament, chamfered corners and incised scrolls, flat, segmental, round and pointed arches and a strange stony boniness that made it unique. The interior was in the same style and key, but was frescoed and highly colored with stained-glass mosaics and marbles. The building is gone but the enigma remains. Why was such a building started in 1882?

We are accustomed in our attempts to clarify American Architecture to date the beginning of Eclecticism with our World's Fair of 1893. However, the architects on either side of the Fire prided themselves on their varied choice of styles. As we look at them sixty years and more after they were built, turned to an even dark grey-brown, they appear remarkably uniform. This is partly on account of their uniform height, five or six stories for commercial buildings and three stories with attic and high basement for residences; and partly because of the popularity of sawn Lemont limestone, Athens marble, we remember, set upright in large slabs—a material peculiar to its time. According to the contemporary boosters, however, these masterpieces were of great variety of styles. We read of "Palladian Italian," of "French Renaissance," of Byzantine, of Venetian, of Lombard, of English, etc.

James W. Sheahan and George P. Upton, associate editors of the *Chicago Daily Tribune*, wrote in 1871, when the city must still have been smoking, a book called *The Great Conflagration*. Their description of the district by wards before its destruction has the value of a newspaper-man's instinct of the significant, and forms an excellent bird's-eye view. The following paragraphs are based on their observations:

"At the time of the Fire, the First Ward, with few exceptions, was of brick and stone—all of the streets were paved. The sidewalks broad and straight, were uniformly of Joliet limestone split in slabs—only a few wooden walks remained. It contained the city and county buildings, the United States Post-Office, Customs House and

Depository. All the banks were in the first ward, all the insurance and real estate buildings, nearly all the whole-sale groceries, drygoods, clothing, hardware—all the hotels except some built since 1869, the Opera House, remodelled at a cost of $90,000, and all the theaters, of which McVicker's had just been re-built.

"During 1869 and 1870, State Street had been improved by thirty to forty marble front business buildings all six stories high, housing many publishers and booksellers. Only two churches remained of the company that once gave Washington Street the name of "Church Row" and dotted Wabash Avenue. There were the Second Presbyterian and St. Mary's, with a convent for the Sisters of Mercy. Along its edge were many factories. Michigan Avenue until a few years before had been a grand place for residences, with Wabash hardly less desirable, but the extension for business was rapidly driving them out—though Terrace Row and Bishop Foley's Palace still remained."

"Bishop's Palace, as it is called, just finished (1855) is perhaps the finest and most princely residence in our city," writes the Chronicler in the *Annual Review* for 1856. It was located on the corner of Michigan and Madison and was built of Athens marble beautifully carved. It had two entrances of a most spacious character; the windows were of plate glass and the frames of cut marble. It was four stories high and cost $22,000. Its architectural proportions are not surpassed by any residence in the West. Van Osdel and Olmstead were the architects.

The most considerable building event that followed the Fire, even exceeding the new Palmer House, was the reconstruction of the City Hall and the County Building, generally known as the Court House. The dignified old Greek Revival building in its remodelled form by Van

ALDINE SQUARE

A residential development of 1874 by Adolph Cudell, architect; recently destroyed

CITY HALL AND COUNTY BUILDING, J. J. EGAN, ARCHITECT, COMPLETED IN 1885

Osdel, had gone down in irretrievable ruin in the holocaust. Its successor was to be chosen by a competition and Otto Matz, as will be brought forth, won the competition for the new building, though he did not build it. Otto Matz died in 1919 on his ninetieth birthday and his son Hermann Matz, so well known to the architects, possesses his father's scrap-books. One of these is devoted to the "great competition," as it was generally called. Perhaps a short account of this huge building-operation, gleaned from Otto's scrap-book, would be more valuable as a prelude than a postlude. As for the accounts of the competition itself Mr. Matz neither dated nor identified his newspaper clippings, but the one describing the sequence of events and on which I am leaning identifies itself as of November or December, 1879, and its type is that of the *Tribune.*

Three days after the Fire (October 11 and 12, 1871) the City Council after arranging for temporary quarters directed the Board of Public works to confer with the Board of Supervisors (who managed County affairs) in regard to the erection jointly of a permanent building in the old location. Eleven days later a wind-fall dropped into the lap of the bereaved city. This was the action of the State Legislature which authorized the payment of $3,000,000 in full of the claim the City had against the State for the Canal improvements. The condition of the gift was that the City should restore the burned bridges and should use the remainder for its share of a new court house. In February, 1872, the Legislature passed a bill authorizing the County Board to issue bonds for $1,500,000 which must build a jail on the North Side and with the remainder build the County's share of the court house.

Matz at this early stage made a design for a joint building which was accepted, but this action was deemed hasty and almost immediately rescinded. In July, 1872, the building committees of the City and the County offered jointly a prize of $5,000 for the best plan, $2,000 for the second best and $1,000 for the third best for a "Municipal Building" and "City Hall." On August 5 the City and County became parties to a contract that in the proposed new building the exterior design should be uniform, each party should light and heat its own half, the expense of the grounds should be equally divided and the County should occupy the east half and the City the west half of the old court house square. In July, 1873, the joint building committee awarded, as a result of the competition, the first prize to Otto H. Matz, the second to Henry L. Gay and the third to Thomas Tilley. This report the City Council accepted with the proviso, however, that this acceptance did not bind them to employ the winner!

The County Board refused to accept the decision of the "Jury" and selected the design of Tilley, and after many meetings and much argument the Council also changed its mind and acquiesced in the appointment of Tilley. Next came the question of the compensation to be paid the architects and that ticklish problem precipitated "another series of rows," which while it established the fee at three percent seems also to have dispossessed the erstwhile fortunate Tilley. The County Board thereupon, completely ignoring the competition, appointed its own architect, J. J. Egan, and the perverse City resurrected Tilley, whose motto apparently was "down but never out." His triumph was short. "Tilley was squeezed out at last and for the past four years has been haunting street corners and places of public resort pouring the story of his grievances into the ears of sympathetic victims of his oratory," says the *Tribune* writer. "He has now pending a suit for some fabulous amount for damages and expects a judgment on the day of Judgment." Our sympathy is decidedly with Tilley.

Whence he came and whither he went I have not been able to discover. He is mentioned apparently only in connection with the designs for the Court House, but there it must be admitted he is mentioned a great deal. After a few more shufflings of the architects, in which the names of Edward Burling and Theodore Karls appear and disappear as associates of Egan and in which incidentally the fee was reduced to two percent, the County Board swore by the nine gods that the work should be begun at once without any further reference to the City authorities. On August 27, 1875, a spadeful of earth was dug out in the presence of a number of City and County officials, who thereupon adjourned to Clem Periolat's "Bean Club, where a goodly portion of them got drunk in honor of the occasion." Farmer Harms was awarded the contract for piling, William S. McNeil & Son the cut-stone, P. J. Sexton the contract for masonry. In the controversy of limestone *versus* granite (spelt "granit" in those days), a compromise was reached, in which limestone for the exterior walls (Lemont for County, Bedford for City) was used and granite for the columns, pilasters and entrances.

Egan, the architect, furnished duplicate drawings and stone details of the façades to the City, but apparently the plan and interior of the Municipal half was worked out by S. D. Cleveland. As built, therefore, the exteriors of the City and County Buildings were identical, but the interiors varied considerably, the municipal side being more lavishly ornamented. The entire building was ready for occupancy at the beginning of 1885 and the cost was in excess of four million. The Court House as a spectacle was a noble pile. The high ceilings, the small window openings and the long corridors made for discomfort and inconvenience; hence its short life—only twenty years— but the exterior was a *tour de force*. For several years as a draughtsman in D. H. Burnham's office I walked along La Salle Street twice a day between the Old Northwestern railway station and the Rookery Building. Never was I tired of gazing at the moldering grandeur of that mighty pile. In the morning its barbarisms were evident enough, but against the evening sky all was forgiven in the rearing silhouette and the cavernous shadows that made the building an incarnation of a Piranesi etching.

This was far better than any of the competition designs and better than any of its Parvenu contemporaries of the seventies when it was conceived. However, it was old-fashioned and out-dated by the time it was finished. Jenney's big windows, Richardson's Romanesque Revival and Burnham's planning had revolutionized big architecture by 1885, and steel construction was just around the corner.

Is it too late to say something about the competition? The accounts of this famous contest as revealed by the Otto Matz scrap-book are not only amusing and interesting but most valuable in their revelation of contemporary taste both of the architect and of the critic. For the newspapers it was a Roman holiday, because very properly the reporters were not allowed at the deliberations of the jury, the Aldermen, the County Commissioners. The competitors and the rival reporters, one of whom crawled down a chimney and thereby executed a scoop, were all thrown to the lions. However, the drawings themselves gave them pause. Civic pride, ignorance of architecture and the grandiose conceptions of the architects filled all with

a healthy respect, and brought forth in the otherwise
caustic comments paeans of extravagant praise.

There is no program of the competition available,
but we know that three prizes were offered—a first of
$5000, second $2000, third $1000. There was no archi-
tectural adviser and, as we know, no guarantee that the
winner would get the job; and we also know that he did
not! Fifty designs were submitted. After many meetings
the joint committee of the Common Council and the
County Commissioner reduced the number to eighteen,
together with their noms de plume, as follows: "Semper
Resurgens"—Rankin and Quensey; "Venetian"—Cochrane and Miller; "Utility"—Rufus Rose; "Marmion"—
C. H. Murdock; "Eureka"—Tilley, Longhurst and Co.;
"Legibus et Populis"—no name; "Let Merit Win"—L. C.
Welsh; "Justitia"—Otto H. Matz; "Star"—York and
Ross; "Avante"—Armstrong and Egan; "Aut Caesar Aut
Nihil"—Henry Lord Gay; "Fitness and Economy"—Bur-
ling and Adler, George H. Edbrook; "Chicago's Pride"—
Theodore Karls; "Urbs in Horto"—Wheelock and
Thomas; "Old Hundred"—S. P. Randall; "Metropolis of
the West"—Bangley of Bloomington; "In Hoc Signo
Vinces"—Dixon and Hamilton.

Otto Matz in that priceless diary of his reproduces contemporary wood-cuts of the winning designs and some of
the "also rans." Almost every one of them is pretty bad,
judged by the fashions of today, and probably none was
very good by the best standard of 1873. But they eloquently reflect the opinion of what constituted monumental architecture sixty-seven years ago in Chicago.
Whatever insults the papers could heap upon the city
and county boards or the temporary Art Gallery in the
Kentucky Building, where the drawings were exhibited

"cold as the bottled airs of winter can make it," they withheld them from the designs themselves, which they regarded with admiration and awe. We note in all of them the extreme elaboration reflecting the prevailing opinion of the profession and of the laity that only by the multiplication of architectural motives and decoration could monumental elegance be acquired. It is evident that, faced with a problem unprecedented in scope and purpose, each competitor hied himself at once to any documents he could find that reproduced the contemporary monumental architecture of Europe. Take, for instance, "Justitia," the winning design by Otto Matz. Its four stories are completely incased with pavilioned façades of round arched windows and superimposed columns or pilasters. Its roof is a high mansard with great square domes on the corner and center pavilions. A domed and columned tower, equally rich, rises from the Washington Street façade. A reviewer writes of it as "a handsome design." A combination of forms from the various periods of the Renaissance with a general adherence to the *pavillon* of the New Louvre, the Hotel de Ville of Paris and the Maison de Commerce of Lyons. The *Times* reporter says, "Among the distinguishing features of the several designs are the French roofs which are treated in a variety of ways from the beautiful to the 'botched.'"

The second prize winner, "Aut Caesar Aut Nihil" by Henry Lord Gay, was perhaps the most original. It was dominated by a tower in the shape of a gigantic Corinthian column, referred to throughout by the critics as the "Shot Tower." The plan was praised by the critics. The third prize design was the famous effort by Thomas Tilley. The building is in the form of a Greek cross set diagonally on the square surmounted by a monstrous dome. It is a mass of re-entrant angles and interfering projections and confused detail. One respects the courage of the jury, but is at a loss to account for their decision.

Boyington's design, which, in a curious communication to the press he either repudiated or transferred the credit of to his associate, Murdock, is very reminiscent of the Reichstag in Berlin, with a huge central tower in a quite different architectural manner, probably his own. One of the best designs, in my opinion, was that submitted by W. L. B. Jenney. It is Venetian-Gothic Style as interpreted in England in Mid-Victorian days by Street or Ruskin. It is reminiscent of the Town Hall in Manchester, as the critics were smart enough to discover. It had two towers, one in the center of the Washington Street façade, and the other of different design on Randolph. The building was simple, however, well proportioned and interesting. The design showing, as might be expected, the greatest native genius is by Edward Burling, submitted by Burling and Adler. The City Hall as built owes it a good deal. The roof was flat for the most part. It was entered approximately on the ground level, and it was obviously well lighted, as it eschewed the great porticoes and cavernous arches, irresistible temptations to most of the competitors. Its principal feature was two towers, one small, one great, on opposite sides. Each of these is a powerful and original composition. A curious side light is the fight, though a very refined one, we may be sure, that Alderman Mahlon O. Ogden, member of the jury, put up for "the design of the Boston architect Sturgis." Sturgis's design was not even among the first eighteen nor can I find it illustrated. I've a feeling, though, that Alderman Ogden may have had excellent reasons. One commentary makes this enlightening observation: " 'Childe Harold' is a Gothic building very handsome in itself but as Gothic architecture is not understood here and only attempted by one or two architects, it is fair to suppose it came from Boston. It is almost ecclesiastical in its treatment, nothing having been modified to suit the modern taste for secular structures. It is really unmeaning in its quaintness to us Chicagoans."

Otto Matz, sound philosopher as well as excellent architect, took his $5000 and his family and went on a grand tour of Europe.

CHAPTER IV

Romance · 1880-1893

ROMANESQUE REVIVAL

AS I look over the episodes in the growth of our city it seems to me that the period from 1880 to the World's Fair in '93, which we have called "Romance," is the most attractive of the lot.

While we are thinking and writing in terms of architecture, nevertheless the growth of the city in size, wealth and prestige brought her to the front rank of American cities. In the decade from 1880 to 1891 her population increased from 503,298 to 1,099,850, her size from 35.79 square miles to 180.2 square miles, her wealth from $117,133,726 to $219,354,368 and her building from $8,207,000 to $47,400,000. Chicago, always front page news from the Fire, what with her growth, her hectic politics, her social problems, now became the true cynosure of the nation in her development of American Architecture. Her gifts in this burgeoning springtime were in the development of the high commercial building, the invention of skeleton construction and its other self, the skyscraper, and the birth of a revolutionary new thought in architecture to bear fruit in the new generation. Certainly enough for only a little more than a decade. The reward for these labors of Hercules was the fair crown of the World's Columbian Exposition.

Looking closer, neither before nor since has an equal *élan vital,* to use a favorite expression of Dr. Cram, possessed our architects, and, if I wanted to stray into other bailiwicks, doubtless our business men and public-spirited citizens as well. I see them then, but I can hardly see them today. Jenney, Burnham, Root, Adler, Sullivan, Beman, Holabird and a score of lesser men—all in a fine frenzy of effort and accomplishment.

Today we stand still and mark time—for what? Sixty years ago we raced headlong to provide shelter for Chicago's miraculous development.

This race was no affair of a smooth straightaway, with all obstacles removed by previous workers; it was an obstacle race of the first water. The obstacles that had to be hurdled or removed were a clay soil which would compress three inches with a load of 4000 pounds to the square foot; a fire hazard with the fresh and lurid memory of the Great Fire and the frank suspicion of the business man that the architect could not build a fireproof structure, and, most serious of all, an inheritance of debased architectural aesthetics. The crisis was obvious; business was on a veritable stampede, realty values were soaring, big and little business was concentrating in the future "Loop"; the architect found himself suddenly not only a necessity but almost a savior. The high building, ten stories and more, was the answer, but how could it be done with only moldy traditions of the past and the equally quaking mud of Chicago to build upon? The architect sat in a game in which his only good card seemed to be the newly invented passenger elevator. How he filled to a straight flush will be the story of this chapter. The first discard had to be the complete scheme of architectural design that had been the fashion from 1855 to 1880. The previous twenty-five years had left as a heritage the worst jumble of illegitimate styles that our country had ever seen. Travesties of the French classic of the second Empire with cast-iron fronts and galvanized-iron cornices, and curious maladaptations of the Victorian Gothic with "Athens marble" slabs and incised "Eastlake" ornament. In this inheritance elaboration and ostentation spelt the "elegance" which was the theme of this Parvenu period of our architecture.

Our architecture of 1880 deserves an enormous amount of credit for completely junking the false ideals and the false pretence of the seventies and apparently without a "by your leave" to their clients. Think of the courage required by the young architects, Burnham and Root, to build the Montauk Block in 1882 of plain brick and with plain walls, with all the white of the famous Palmer House in its panoply of columns, cornices and domes only a block or two away. However, the Chicago architects did not grapple unaided with the question of "style." As a matter of fact, they joined forces with the crusade which came out of Boston about 1887. The crusade was called the Romanesque Revival, and its Coeur de Lion was H. H. Richardson. Fighting in the East singled handed at first, he found his principal lieutenants in the men of Chicago. And they found his basic style, the Romanesque, an excellent base in their attack on their special problem—the design of the tall building. We will find that it wasn't the only influence, but it was predominant enough, especially in the design of monumental structures, to give its name to the period.

Whoever invented the name "Romanesque Revival" I do not know, but it is contemporary. It stuck and was certainly a well known and popular title in my college days. It was so much in my ears that I imagined nearly every building between 1880 and the World's Fair of

1893 had round arches and the ornamental earmarks of mediaeval France, and furthermore was sired directly or indirectly by Henry Hobson Richardson. Perhaps the fact that I studied architecture looking Trinity Church in the face in Copley Square had something to do with it. In truth my first attempt to write this chapter commenced with a biography of the great Richardson.

He chose the Romanesque style of Southern France for his vehicle because he considered it basic "good earth" in which American seeds could germinate. The style made an instantaneous appeal and spread like wild fire, especially in the West. It made its slightest impress in New York City, but in the New England States, the Middle West and the South it was dominant. It was surprising to see in Washington, the home of the Classic, so many Romanesque examples. Richardson was soon hailed as America's greatest architect. He continued to design exclusively in the style and soon acquired a following of young and vigorous designers. Of all this more later.

We have spoken of other influences. Considering the great fame of the Romanesque Revival, it is surprising to find that of the buildings erected in Chicago between 1879 and 1893, the Romanesque was actually outnumbered by another mode. If one includes frame houses, by far the largest proportion belong stylistically in the category of the contemporary and much derided Queen Anne, of which also more later.

There was still another manner, the name of which has faded but which sixty years ago was dear to Chicago architects because they considered that they invented it, and that was the "Commercial Style." This was a common sense manner, carefully worked out in brick and terra cotta as the appropriate dress for the "Elevator Building," also something very new. Elevator buildings

were structures of six to ten stories which appeared about
1878 with the introduction of the passenger elevator and
continued to 1887, when they were rendered obsolescent
by the establishment of skeleton construction. All these
styles and manners constituted a romantic and adventurous attitude toward architecture and toward life itself.
I think of their authors in terms of youth, virility, courage
and confidence. These were in truth the builders of
Chicago.

Those of my age were brought up in the tradition that
Henry Hobson Richardson was the greatest architect
America had produced. This tradition still obtains,
although there is a growing indication that another generation will transfer the palm to Louis Sullivan.

I have had doubts at times as to the authenticity of the
Richardson legend—that perhaps his genius, or call it
his personality, which is said to have completely hypno-
tized his contemporaries, had wrought the same spell over
posterity; however, when one reads contemporary accounts of his deeds and influence the doubts vanish.
Robert McLean, whose brilliant editorship of the *Western Architect* illuminates the Romantic age, says this
in 1886, among many things, concerning Richardson's
power: "Architecture in the United States is in a transitional state. It is possible that a distinctive American
style may be the result. Richardson's death dramatized
the Romanesque. Victorian Gothic and Queen Anne will
alike disappear before the Richardsonian Romanesque in
all degrees and varieties of adaption, imitation and appro-
priation. Hitherto the style of American architecture has
on the whole been English, somewhat out of date, much
as the fashions in this country used Parisian a few seasons
before. Richardson's taste, associations and training
were distinctly French. His genius seems to have severed

American architecture from English precedent. He has apparently taken the place which Charles Eastlake and Norman Shaw occupy in England. Our Romanesque Revival may yet affect England!" [1] And again, "He is recognized by his compeers as the foremost architect in America." Mrs. Schuyler Van Rensselaer, his biographer, tries to explain his immediate and nationwide popularity by saying that "Richardson in expressing his personal taste unconsciously expressed the taste of the American people." She ends her biography with praise as extravagant as that used by MacLean: "We may call him with confidence, not only the greatest American artist but the greatest benefactor of American art who has yet been born."

If I may make a guess as to the nationwide acceptance of the Romanesque Revival I would pin it all on Trinity Church. Brattle Street Church, Boston, older than Trinity and also Romanesque, caused no sensation. But in Trinity a magnificent exterior was followed through with an equally beautiful interior. Stained glass windows by Burne-Jones, mural decorations by John La Farge and every detail by an artist-craftsman was something that the American public hadn't seen for fifty years, if ever. Twenty years wandering in the Parvenu desert, and Trinity was a lush oasis! Hence the Romanesque Revival.

An artist's reputation with posterity depends on the vividness of his personality, on the power and popularity of his work, and most of all on the influence that he wielded on his contemporaries and on his successors. If his power was so great that he changed, as in this case, the course of architecture, creating a new expression which the people accepted, then he becomes one of the immortals. The men who have done this in America are Thomas Jefferson,

[1] *Inland Architect*, VII, 36.

Benjamin Latrobe, H. H. Richardson, Charles F. McKim, and Louis Sullivan.

It has been the habit, in order to drive home a point in an architectural homily, to stress homogeneity far more than it deserves. Since the end of Georgian days, or at least after the high point of the Greek Revival, there had always been a certain eclecticism which introduced at the will of architect or builder styles and forms alien to the fashion of the time. Nevertheless similarity of methods of construction, building materials, purpose and aging give all buildings of the same period, in any one land, a family appearance regardless of technicalities of style or the originality of the builder. This is true of the buildings between 1880 and 1893.

Though the Queen Anne or Free Classic style has outnumbered the Romanesque Revival in its examples, nevertheless the inherent power of the latter, the great buildings whose guise it bore and perhaps, most of all, the fame of its author have fastened its name on the period. So again, what was the Romanesque Revival, and who was Richardson?

Romanesque architecture in its broadest aspect is the architecture of Europe from the fall of Rome to the beginning of the thirteenth century. It is one of the three great basic historic styles—Classic, Romanesque, Gothic. It had great variations depending on its geography and on its chronology. In the Near East in Byzantium and in Venice and other eastern Italian cities it was a thing of color through its marbles and mosaics and its gorgeous interiors. In Central Italy, where we call it the Tuscan, the many storied leaning Tower and the marble façades of Pisa, Prato and Pistoija show it in a rare mood of marbled playfulness. Farther north in Milan and Bologna we find Romanesque buildings stern and joyless but virile with the germ of future structural development. In Germany the Romanesque has given us the great Rhenish brick churches. In England the tremendous fanes built by the Conqueror are Romanesque, though called Norman, and the Saxons used the style before him. In France, as one might expect, the style reaches its greatest beauty. At Arles and Nîmes, Angouleme, Perigueux, Vizille and Cluny, we have the Romanesque in a perfect relationship of design, sculpture and construction. In Spain, France was obviously the model, but the Spaniards added a drama and exuberance all their own. It is interesting to know that the first example of Romanesque architecture that captured the imagination of our people was this same Spanish Romanesque, for Richardson in the tower of Trinity Church, Boston, took the cathedral of Salamanca as his inspiration and *point de départ.*

Now who was Richardson? Henry Hobson Richardson began as the handsome and talented son of a wealthy southern family. He was born in Louisiana in 1838. He went to Harvard where he was a sort of wonder youth excelling in nearly every activity. In 1860 he was admitted to the Ecole des Beaux Arts in Paris, famous architectural school and mother of schools. Unable to return home on account of the Civil War and with the family fortunes swept away, he entered the office of a distinguished French architect, Labrouste. Labrouste, a brilliant innovator and functionalist, had a decided influence on the architecture of his time in England and in America, as well as in his mother country. The war over, Richardson returned and practiced first in New York and a little later in Boston which was ever after his home. There he died in April, 1886, of a disease which Mrs. Van Rensselaer, with the quaint prudery of the time, calls "his chronic ailment." It was in reality nothing more immodest than Bright's disease.

In 1877 he finished Trinity Church in Boston. He built it in the Romanesque style, which he had previously tried out in the nearby Brattle Street Church. The great size of Trinity and the reputation of its famous rector, Phillips Brooks, doubtless had something to do with its extraordinary power, but, most of all, its magnificent architecture made it almost over night the most talked of building in America. Architects, particularly the younger men, began to imitate Richardson and to enlist under his banner for a better architecture, which to them meant buildings in the Romanesque style. By 1885 from Maine to California it was the accepted and fashionable mode, particularly for large buildings where stone would normally be employed and for churches, where it almost completely ousted the Gothic. Richardson erected four buildings in Chicago. One was very early (more properly by Gambrill and Richardson), 1872, one of the phoenixes rising from the flames. It had the very considerable name of the American Merchants Union Express Company. Mrs. Van Rensselaer praises it and says that it had Romanesque motives. So does the Chicago architect P. B. Wight, who says that it had both segmental and pointed arches. However, no known picture of the building exists, although several living architects remember it—Arthur Woltersdoff and Richard E. Schmidt both described it to me. It stood where now is an elevator garage, opposite the Majestic Theatre. P. B. Wight had charge of its erection. According to witnesses, it was not Romanesque at all but of the Victoria Gothic persuasion, much like the work that Richard M. Hunt was doing in New York.

The other three were better known, in fact famous. One of them, the Field Wholesale, 1885, wantonly (it seems to me) destroyed in 1930, was internationally famous. The third, the MacVeagh house, 1885, razed in 1914, was not famous at all. As Richardson died in April, 1886, the buildings were completed by his successors Shepley, Rutan and Coolidge, who probably designed some of the interior finish; certainly this was the case in the Glessner House. All of these three will be described in their proper categories.

Now that we have laid the foundation, with considerable effort, consisting of H. H. Richardson and his Romanesque style, let us see what the Chicago architects built upon it. The first most important and most interesting problem which they tackled was the high building demanded by business, necessitated by the high cost of land and recently made practicable by the newly invented passenger elevator. The architects of Chicago accepted the challenge with enthusiasm, energy and ingenuity. The first protagonist to appear in the lists was the Montauk Building. To indulge in hyperbole, what Chartres was to the Gothic Cathedral the Montauk Block was to the high commercial building. Its young architects, Burnham and Root, had very little precedent when in 1881 they were given the job.

The typical office building of the time was a five to six story building of very ornate Classic or Victorian Gothic style, a cast-iron front or an Athens marble façade or, in case of the Gothic, a brick and stone exterior, and a galvanized-iron cornice for all of them. It was semi-fireproof. Its construction was of solid masonry walls. The floor was of brick arches or often of wood beams protected by thin terra cotta slabs nailed on their bottom sides, and the supports were cast-iron columns unprotected. The foundations were of stepped-off dimension footings isolated in the important examples after the theories of Frederick

THE MONTAUK BLOCK, BURNHAM AND ROOT,
ARCHITECTS, BUILT IN 1882

Baumann. It usually, as in the First National Bank Building next door to the Montauk, had steps from the sidewalk leading up to the main or first floor and steps leading
down to the low-ceilinged ground floor. The comparison
of the two neighbors, one, the First National, built in
1881-82 on the site of the post-office and Haverley's
Theater after the Fire and the Montauk illustrate the
daring of Burnham and the originality of Root. The building shows ten stories identical above the second, except
for a slight variation in the brick work above the segmental window heads at alternate stories. All of the brick
is separated at window-sill levels by thin terra cotta
bands. The cornice is simplicity itself, of brick and terra
cotta with very slight projection. The entrance to the
ground floor shops is at the side-walk level, but the
approach to the main floor and the elevators is up a
flight of steps inside an open archway. The construction
is of solid walls resting on isolated "floating" rafts constructed of crossed iron rails in a concrete slab. The floors
were of terra cotta tiles. The building cost $200,000.

Why is the Montauk so important? It introduced the
following innovations, each a permanent step in the
advance of Chicago architecture. In style it was as functional as Louis Sullivan ever dared advocate and far more
functional than any of his work at the time or for some
time after. It was in fact, the father of a style called by
Chicago architects "The Commercial Style," which in
four or five years merged into the Romanesque. *Industrial Chicago* describes it as having "Romanesque
ornament." The use of "floating foundations," a broad
raft of concrete reinforced with iron rails, used here for
the first time, revolutionized foundation construction and
remained the accepted form until caissons were first used
in 1892. It was the first thoroughly fireproof high building

in Chicago because in it the columns were protected for the first time,[2] and finally it was the first building in which work continued unabated through the winter, as the area was covered with a canvas tent and heated. The pioneer Montauk was wrecked when the present First National Bank was built but its soul goes marching on.

The architectural progeny of the Montauk were at once numerous and of a type: I am calling them "elevator buildings." And again we need a definition, because all sorts of buildings were being built in the boom between 1880 and 1890. Let us eliminate, therefore, all buildings below six or seven stories which might or might not have elevators, and let us eliminate warehouses, manufacturing buildings, etc., confining our term only to "office-buildings." "Elevator buildings" are, therefore, high office-buildings of solid masonry construction.

ELEVATOR BUILDINGS

The elevator buildings which once ruled the roost in Chicago existed between, say, 1879 and 1889. As has been said, they were called into being by a lively increase in prosperity, continued concentration of business in the Loop, and sky-rocketing values of real estate, all of which put the architects on the spot and also found them on their toes, with only their enthusiasm and ingenuity to guide them and only their inexperience to hold them. Elevator buildings flourished to the astonishment of the world until then and were given the *coup de grace* by the invention of skeleton construction and its demonstration in the Tacoma Building in 1889. There seems to have been a concentration of them along south La Salle and about

---

[2] *Industrial Chicago* II, 387, says, speaking of the advent of the high building, "The first of them, the Montauk, was finished in 1882. This class of structure is distinguished by masonry walls enclosing fireproof interiors."

the Board of Trade where still may be found, with their heads unbowed, the Rookery, the Austin, the Rialto, etc. There is another group of survivors in the wholesale district in the vicinity of Jackson and Market. The buildings are all about ten stories high, which was the practical limit for a building with solid masonry walls. They are all built of red pressed brick and trimmed with red or brown terra cotta. They all have windows as large as possible of the newly perfected plate glass. In style, they were really notable in casting off so suddenly the popular extravagancies of the previous decade and in originating and developing an expression simple, dignified and above all functional. Its details can doubtless be found in various architectural books such as Raguenet, but its ensemble is, as far as I can see, unprecedented. At any rate they thought they had something and called it the "Commercial Style." As John Root said, "Living in the full light of the nineteenth century, freed from the thralldom of our less fortunate brothers across the sea, we men can do what we please." [3]

As the fame of Richardson's Romanesque Revival increased, the "Commercial Style" shed much of its austerity, and its latest examples were enriched with Romanesque ornament, but they never lost their character as the shock troops of the American skyscraper.

Perhaps the best way to discuss the elevator building will be to mention categorically some of the important ones following the Montauk:

CALUMET BUILDING. Built in 1882–1883 by Burnham and Root, had the distinction of being the first high building in the "new Board of Trade district" and the second high building in Chicago, having been built directly after the Montauk. It was of St. Louis red brick and in the

[3] Speech at dinner of the Western Society of Architects, November 18, 1886.

Romanesque style. One authority claims it was "the first building in the World where fireclay was used for ceilings and hollow tile for partitions."

FIRST NATIONAL BANK. Any collection of photographs of the effects of the Chicago Fire is pretty sure to show the mostly ruined post-office building on the northwest corner of Dearborn and Monroe which later was the site of the First National Bank of 1882. In style it, like the Board of Trade, was an anachronism, as it harked back almost to pre-Fire days for its models, ignoring the new light set forth by the Montauk. It had a basement with descending steps from the sidewalk and it had the ascending steps from the sidewalk to the main floor. It was designed in the Classic style with superimposed orders divided into a cadence of one, two and three stories with a huge Classic cornice. The building was of stone and brick. The Classic style was used, it must be said, with much more skill and knowledge than characterized the Parvenu buildings of the seventies. Nevertheless the voice is the voice of Jacob. The architects were Burling & Whitehouse.

PULLMAN BUILDING. Here is a splendid early example of the "Elevator Building" ready for one's inspection. It has scarcely been changed except for the new huge plate glass store front that cleverly conceals the supporting granite columns and piers on the Michigan and Adams fronts. The building is nine stories and attic, its ground dimensions of one hundred twenty seven by one hundred seventy feet. It is of granite and brick and cost nearly a million. The architect was S. S. Beman, who designed it at the early age of 27 years in 1883, which fact is inserted in the shield on Michigan Avenue. Although the inspired editor of *Industrial Chicago* calls it "American Norman Gothic," it is one of our earliest examples of the Romanesque Revival, seasoned a bit with Queen

Anne. This commentator in a lengthy description also says, "At the level of the fifth story, three Marat turrets spring from corbels while the rounded northeast corner of the building is capped by oillettes and a cove roof"— a picturesque description in a picturesque age. This great building, the most important office building in the city when built, created a profound impression and was justly admired especially for its grandiose arched portals. It is a splendid commentary on the quality of fashion, which enthralls one generation only to be repudiated by the next.

COUNSELMAN BUILDING (*Destroyed*). Burnham and Root followed up their Calumet Building with the Counselman Building on the northwest corner of La Salle and Jackson. We must not let the creative power of Louis Sullivan blind us to the equal originality of John Root. Sullivan was striving after light, but at the time he was experimenting with exuberant ornament applied often wherever he could find room for it. Root, with remarkable courage and taking great chances, put the ornamental side of his art behind him for the nonce and threw his soul into a functional expression of this new intensely Chicago problem, which meant solving problems of planning, foundations, fireproofing and utilities. One feels this intense earnestness about this building long since gone. The building was ten stories—but let us quote a contemporary description: "The first story is constructed of Jonesborough, dark rose rock faced granite and the superstructure of Anderson Pressed brick (plain and molded) and the Northwestern Company's terra cotta. Within, the floors were constructed of eight inch hollow tile arches, the partitions of three and a half inch hollow tile. The roof covered with flat glazed tiles in Portland cement" instead of the usual slate. "Fireproof suspended ceilings also mark this building." The building, one hundred forty-five feet high, shows little exterior ornamentation, the architects adopting instead the idea of massiveness and durability.[4] Root in the façade uses, as he often did, one of those subtle cadences which must have been inspired by his work as a musician. Beginning at the top of the ground story the beat is 1-2-1-2-1-2. Almost waltz time. The building makes another step in advance by eliminating all exterior steps.

MALLERS BUILDING. As a young man I knew John J. Flanders. I knew him as the architect of the Board of Education. He always spoke not only modestly but deprecatingly of his work when I tried to draw him out. He spoke of himself as a star of very low magnitude in the galaxy of which John Root was the chief. I did not know at the time that he was the architect of the Mallers Building, which stood at the southwest corner of Quincy and La Salle, yet this building when built in 1884 when Flanders was about 35, was the highest in Chicago— twelve stories and one of the best. Its round turret-like corner looked admirable in its location and its rich cornice and arcaded upper three stories, while perhaps not as functional as some of the other elevator buildings, made an impressive monument, and it still clung to the few exterior steps and a depressed ground floor. It was one of the stalwarts and, physically at least, a head above any of them. Flanders was born in Chicago in 1848 of a father who settled here in '34. He learned his profession in the offices of August Bauer, Wadskier and Edward Burling and opened an office in 1874. The Haven, Andersen, Brainard, Healy and Hoyne schools were among his works.

[4] *Industrial Chicago*, I, 183.

PHOENIX—ONCE WESTERN UNION, NOW AUSTIN.   Still
another building by Burnham and Root was and is the
Austin Building known also at various times as the
Phoenix and the Western Union. It has a commanding
position on the south side of Jackson between La Salle
and Clark. It is eleven stories in height, and here Root
again has brilliantly experimented with the novel and
baffling problem of the high building. His cadence here is
1-1-1-3-1-2-1. As in the Rialto he used an encircling balcony near the top, and he anticipates the moderns by
completely avoiding a projecting cornice. The detail is
masterly and in vigorous and consistent scale. The
sprightly commentator in *Industrial Chicago* sees in it
"Indian Mongolian and European," in fact anything but
Romanesque. Nevertheless it is Romanesque of a kind
and an excellent example. The only evidence of a sweet
tooth is the encircling balcony at the tenth floor and the
slightly projecting bay windows from the fourth to the
seventh floors. Root, I believe, never used either again
on an office building. It is interesting to see how the
exuberant Root has treated every story in a slightly different way and yet has not belied the function of any of
them—shops on the ground, a bank above and offices
from there up. Root was a master of material and never
did he use it more skillfully than here. In the Phoenix
perhaps for the first time the mediaeval remnants of sidewalk steps up or down are entirely eliminated and there
is no depressed ground floor.

ROOKERY.   The Rookery was the next great office
building. It stood and stands at the southeast corner of
La Salle and Adams. It was built in 1885 and the architects were Burnham and Root. This was the site of the
old City Hall and water tank—"The old barrack and
rat den of '72 to '82." It is lighted on four sides by streets

and alleys, and in the center is a great court yard glazed
at the third story level. When I started my career, I was
a draughtsman for D. H. Burnham and Co., and the
office was in the Rookery. Edward Waller, who conceived
the Rookery and remained its guiding genius during his
long life, told me at that time that here was developed
the modern office building plan. Certainly it was a great
step in advance, and in the size of offices, width of corridors, disposition of utilities, banking of the elevators,
etc., established standards most of which still prevail.
The best proof of Edward Waller's remark is that the
Rookery still proudly holds its head erect and keeps step
certainly in popularity and rentals with its towering and
streamlined descendants. The architectural design of the
Rookery was far in advance of its immortal neighbor, the
Home Insurance Building. As in its neighbor the first two
stories are of granite. Above, the sequence of stories is
2-2-3-3-1, eleven stories in all, all in brick and terra cotta.
Its glory is its magnificent crown—a parapet, not a cornice, with corner pinnacles and powerful and rich decoration. That difficult and indescribable thing called "scale"
by us architects is handled in a masterly way. The "style"
of the Rookery was a source of wonder and much discus-
sion with its contemporaries. The illustration in *Industrial
Chicago* is labeled "Indo-Roman ornament," while the
description says, "It is all treated with the richness of
India and Venice but observing still the horizontal-
vertical forms which puzzle the Roman, the South and
East Indian alike," all nonsense of course. The ornament
is East Indian as translated by Root's fervid and fanciful
pencil.

Standing in the Rookery I looked out over the beautiful
courtyard, four square, above the iron and glass roof of
the "hall of lost steps," as the French would say. It seemed

unbelievable that the slender enamelled brick piers and the ochre terra cotta bands all embroidered with a vigorous arabesque could be of solid masonry construction. The engineer of the building got out for me photostats of the original plans, and we found that this court was of skeleton construction. Each pier contained a square cast-iron column joined to the next by a ten inch beam, an eight inch channel and an angle flush with the face of the column which last supported the brick facing. Coming only two years after the Home Insurance and a year or more before the Tacoma, it must have been the first building to have utilized Major Jenney's great invention, but in the court only. Another thing shown me by the engineer was the alley and Quincy elevations. These are solid masonry like the street fronts but only above the third floor. One story in the basement and two above ground are composed of huge double cast-iron columns, dumbbell fashion, which carry the vast load of masonry wall above.

The Rookery is John Root at his very best. An improvisation in tones and harmonies both delicate and strong, spontaneity of expression with profundity of thought, all fashioned with the inspiration of genius.

The beautiful entrance halls and elevator grilles in white and gold were added later, and, believe it or not, are by Frank Lloyd Wright.

There were other elevator buildings—the Gaff on La Salle near Quincy by S. V. Shipman, the Royal Insurance by Boyington on Jackson next the Mallers, the C. B. and Q. office building northeast corner of Adams and Franklin, etc.—but enough of them. They were really curtain raisers anyway, all except one, and that was the Monadnock Block. The Monadnock is famous on several counts. It was the greatest of all elevator buildings and the last "skyscraper" to be built of solid masonry construction. There was a widely current story, doubtless true, that the French savants in '93 turned their backs on the glories of the Court of Honor to gaze in wonder at the soaring flanks of the Monadnock. This they thought fulfilled their hopes of seeing an "American Style of Achitecture." Everyone knows that this building, all of brick, raises its sixteen stories at the southwest corner of Clark and Jackson. The accounts of its magnificent simplicity vary slightly. Probably John Root's sister-in-law Harriet Monroe tells the most authentic one. She says that Owen Aldis, representative of the Brooks Estate of Boston, the owners and heavy investors in Chicago realty, objected to the preliminary designs of Root as being too ornate. Root went on a vacation and during his absence his partner Burnham directed the building to be designed as a great masonry block without ornament. Root, disgusted and sceptical at first, was soon to scent the dramatic possibilities. Flaring it out like an Egyptian pylon at top and bottom and adding the carefully proportioned bays, he achieved a triumph. William Dutton, who was foreman of the office at the time, told me that he suggested chamfering the corners beginning at nothing at the base and ending with a slice about four feet wide at the top. This clever device gives the illusion of sloping walls at a minute fraction of the expense. This chamfer it was said was so costly for the Anderson Press Co., who had to make different shaped brick for every fourth course, that it nearly put them out of business. There is another story to be told of the choice of construction. When the Monadnock was built the Home Insurance was five years old and the Tacoma was aged two; the Manhattan and the Fair Store had been started. All of these were of skeleton construction. The Brooks Estate of Boston was too conservative to trust the new-fangled steel skeleton just invented in Chicago. When the thickness of the walls at the Monadnock at the ground story, some seven feet, is considered and the enormous weight on the foundation, no wonder that the elevator building was quietly laid away.

STUDEBAKER BUILDING.   If this building had been built two years later instead of in 1886 it doubtless would have been of skeleton construction. The architect, S. S. Beman, achieved the goal of the architects of the time, big windows, by constructing his piers of granite, which on account of its enormous strength enabled him to reduce their diameters and widths. It received tremendous acclaim probably on account of novel appearance and its aforesaid big windows. The arches running through three stories have little relationship to the stories above, and for a masonry building the corners are woefully weak. In fact there was great excitement when in 1891 the southern corners and adjoining wall had to be elevated eight inches, for the heavy hand of the mighty Auditorium next door had pulled it down that much in the muck.

One naturally asked, "What was Louis Sullivan doing while Burnham and Root were astonishing the natives and the nation with their tremendous structures and Root was evolving his functional treatment of the high building?" Sullivan became the partner of Adler in 1881. He was six years younger than Root. As a draughtsman in Adler's office he had designed the Borden Block in 1879 at the northwest corner of Randolph and Dearborn. As a new member of Adler and Sullivan he designed the Revell Building at the northeast corner of Adams and Wabash, standing, 1881-83; the Ryerson Building, 1884, just east of the Masonic Temple, razed in 1939; the Troescher Building, 15 S. Market, standing, 1884; the Dexter Building, 640 S. Wabash, 1887, standing; and others. It is doubtful if any of these buildings would qualify as high buildings, as none exceeded six stories in height and only one, the Ryerson Building, seems to be strictly an office building and therefore not within the limits of our definition of elevator buildings. However, any chronicler who ignores any considerable work of Sullivan is skating on thin ice. Adler and Sullivan were not building any high office-buildings at this time, probably because none came into the office. That is unfortunate because it would have been interesting to see what Louis Sullivan would have done with a twelve-story elevator building. Could he have improved on John Root? I don't believe it.

In the design of those listed above Sullivan seems to be attempting two things. First to increase the window area which he did by greatly thickening the piers from front to back and spanning the space between the piers at each floor by a steel or iron face, which we architects call a "spandrel." This spandrel might be supported with one or two upright ornamental iron members called "mullions." By this brilliant method, used by other architects as well, the number of piers was lessened by nearly half, and the glass area correspondingly increased. To put it very simply, the façades of commercial buildings in the fifties and early sixties had been flat masonry walls punched with holes for windows in uniform order. In the later sixties and seventies after, as well as before, the Fire, windows were still of uniform size and uniformly distributed, but each window was separated from its fellow by an ornamental pier, a column. What the architects of the eighties did—Sullivan, Jenney and the rest—was to bundle these piers together and fill in the wide spaces left between with windows separated perhaps with the aforementioned iron mullions. The foundations of these

piers were "isolated" after the Baumann principle, either
on John Root's floating concrete rafts, or on the old
fashioned pyramids of stone. The interiors were either
of fireproof construction, cast-iron columns with hollow
tile arches, of "mill" heavy timber construction, or wood
joists with terra cotta block protection.

We have gone so far afield after Sullivan's first objective
that we have nearly forgotten his second which was to
invent some new system of ornament that would not
depend on any historic style. This theory of Sullivan's—
that America should have an indigenous expression in
architecture—was doubtless conceived, mulled over, if
not worked out in endless discussions, with his friend John
Edelmann over many a pipe and mug of beer in all sorts
of places, the most interesting of which was Edelmann's
"hangout," a house boat on the Calumet River. If you
care to see some of the work of this exuberant personality,
who cast a spell over the younger Louis, examine the
elevator grilles and balustrade of the Pullman Building
done by Edelmann, according to Sullivan's biographer.[5]

This new "style" of Sullivan (and Edelmann) seems
to have been based on Egyptian motives and appears
consistently until Sullivan fell for the nonce under the
influence of Richardson in the Auditorium only to emerge
with his fully developed philosophy and system of ornament in the Transportation Building of the World's Fair.

Of these early buildings of Adler and Sullivan the
Borden was the earliest, 1879. It had a naïve story
sequence of 2-2-2 with a great lunette (half moon) of
ornament topping each bay. The Revell Building (remodelled) has the same lunettes and more of the spiny
Egyptoid ornament. The Troescher Building has glass at
a maximum and a curiously illogical bedstead upper story,

[5] Hugh Morrison, *Louis Sullivan*, p. 59.

with a further development of his experimental ornamentation, coming to a head in his Ryerson Building on
Randolph, which it seems to me is the worst building
Sullivan ever did. Apparently he thought so too, for in
the Dexter Building he practically abandons all ornament
and adopts a base, shaft and cap sequence 1-4-1, rare then
but the accepted arrangement, after the World's Fair of
'93, for all styles of buildings.

The Dexter Building, severely plain, was started with the
Auditorium but was finished long before, and it is significant as a full pause, a stop for breath before he plunges
into the new world of his philosophy and accomplishment.

Sullivan, like all the others, was profoundly impressed
by Richardson's Field Wholesale. We have read, or will
read, what he said about it. But the rarest compliment
he could pay it was to imitate it or, more properly, be
influenced by its example, and this occurred in two great
buildings, the Walker Warehouse, 200 South Market, and
the Auditorium. This author, admirer of Sullivan as he
is, cannot see the supreme virtues of his ecstatic biographer, who claims it is superior to the great creation
of Richardson. To this writer it looks hard, gaunt and
bony. The gigantic entrance arches mean little and dwarf
the great size of the building, a full city block. They and
the huge adjoining windows are out of scale with each
other and with the remainder of the building. The masterpiece of Richardson left you uplifted with its majesty
and wet-eyed with its beauty. Personal experience records
no such effect of the Walker Warehouse. Such, however,
cannot be said about Adler and Sullivan's greatest work
in size and fame, the Auditorium.

THE AUDITORIUM.   By all odds the most spectacular
and the greatest, at least in point of size of the elevator
buildings, if it can be so called, was the Auditorium.

THE AUDITORIUM, ADLER AND SULLIVAN, ARCHITECTS, DEDICATED IN 1889

Viewed from the southwest

The commentator in *Industrial Chicago* for once hits the nail on the head when he says that the Auditorium was to the Chicago of 1891 what the Palmer House was to the city of the seventies. It not only inflated the pride of the citizenry well nigh to the bursting point, but its importance and fame soon jumped over local limitations, and the great building became first of national and then of international significance. All of this redounded greatly to the reputation of the city, for now magnificence and culture shone forth unmistakably where once the world fancied it saw only mud and pig-sticking. Certainly it was an important factor in the choice of Chicago for the World's Columbian Exposition in 1893.

The architects of this vast enterprise were Adler and Sullivan. I like to think of the building as more the creation of the senior partner. Sullivan came into his own later as leader and prophet with the Transportation Building at the World's Fair. At the Auditorium he stands on the threshold and seems to be trying to divine the sign in the sky. At the moment he is a follower with the other young men in the train of Richardson notwithstanding his accomplishments in creative design in the Troescher and Ryerson Buildings. He threw them overboard when faced with the tremendous responsibility of designing the Auditorium. So in the eighties Sullivan became a convert, along with the rest, to the Romanesque Revival, though he never would admit it. His Auditorium Building in Chicago stands, as far as the exterior is concerned, as one of the best examples of this style, yet there is no suggestion in the form of this building of its primary function in the housing of a vast auditorium. In fact, its great tower seems to preclude the possibility of a huge hall lying beyond. May I quote myself? [6]

[6] *The Story of Architecture in America.*

"The Auditorium Building reeks with personalities. Within its granite portals have come the great of the land and of all lands. The most brilliant of the song-birds of opera have fluttered and caroled within this stony cage; rulers, statesmen, captains of industry as visitors to the great exposition or the opera have here been entertained. To the lover of architecture it is an absorbing artistic document. Into it went Louis Sullivan, one of the crowd, a practitioner of the vernacular, understood and beloved by everyone; out of it came Sullivan, the mystic, an apostle of a new creed, unto the public a stumbling block and unto his profession foolishness.

"It took several years to build the Auditorium Building. As in other buildings, the plans having been made and the specifications written, the construction was well under way before it was necessary to work out the details for decorative or ornamental portions, especially those of the great Auditorium itself, and it was in this interval that the metamorphosis of Sullivan occurred. The great Romanesque granite façade might have been by Richardson or Root, but come within, examine the carvings on the maple finish of what was once the bar and is now one again, go into the huge Auditorium, look up at the misty ceiling with its rhythmic recessional of mighty arches, study the golden grilles on either side of the proscenium— in short, wherever there is ornamentation you will observe that this is no longer Romanesque, but something quite different. Where the Romanesque was material, this is ethereal; where the old was of common and brutal forms, this is of fairy-land—the germ and the beginning of life, the tender shoots pushing their way up through the softening sod, the twining tendrils and the bursting bud. 'O soft Melodious Springtime, first-born of life and love,' wrote Sullivan on the wall. Through this vernal symphony runs another motive, geometrical and cold, frost patterns on the pane, snow crystals on a black sleeve, dew glistening on forsaken webs. 'A great life has passed into the tomb, and there awaits the requiem of winter's snows.'

"This is not rhetoric or fine writing. Sullivan actually attempted a plastic symbolization of such thoughts, and as he read them into his design we, if we are sympathetic and discerning, can read them out. It is therefore in the Auditorium Building that Sullivan broke with conformity and became a knight errant on his own, a Galahad. No more Romanesque came from his hand after that building."

What had given the architects of Chicago pause in their uncertainty was the advent of Richardson in their midst and the building of his greatest achievement, the Marshall Field Wholesale, in 1885-87. Sullivan not only admired it but imitated it. The upper six stories of the Auditorium, not counting the tower, are very similar to the Field Wholesale, and the massiveness of the lower stories and the feeling of stone built for eternity certainly stems from Richardson and characterizes other contemporary work of Sullivan.[7] The style was admittedly Romanesque.

There is another theory about the massiveness and absence of ornamentation from the Auditorium, and this comes direct from Paul Mueller who was Adler's engineer during the drawing of the plans and the construction of the building. Mueller himself told me that the working plans were well nigh finished for a highly ornamental façade replete with bays and oriel windows. However, a remark of John Root was repeated to Sullivan, to the effect that "Louis couldn't build an honest wall without

[7] The story sequence of the Field Wholesale is 1-3-2-1. That of the Auditorium 1-1-1-4-2-1.

covering it with ornament." Sullivan was furious and, in order to show Root that he could, the nearly finished plans were discarded, according to Mueller, and what we now see resulted. The second preliminary design published by Morrison in his *Louis Sullivan* more or less bears out the story. Perhaps the most important reason for simplicity was both the admiration of the director for the Field Wholesale and their insistence that the cost be kept down.

Quoting Morrison, "The construction of the Auditorium took three years. The site finally acquired was an irregular plot on the south half of the block bounded by Michigan, Congress, Wabash and Van Buren Streets, with a total of 63,500 square feet. . . . . Excavation was begun on January 28, 1887. . . . ." The building was dedicated by a great performance on December 9, 1889, at which were present the President of the United States, Governor Fifer and his suite, Ferdinand Peck whose brain child the whole project was, etc., etc. The greatest attraction of all was Adelina Patti, who sang "Home Sweet Home." Her performance demonstrated the superb acoustics of the great Auditorium Theatre. But why copy as I would be tempted to do the very complete account of the Auditorium in Morrison's *Louis Sullivan?*

Let me rather recount certain basic causes and effects and recommend the reader to more complete sources. First the Auditorium owed its being to the very daring attempt of Ferdinand Peck and other public spirited citizens to give grand opera to Chicago in the Old Exposition Building on Michigan Avenue, where now stands the Art Institute. This was for the Spring Festival of 1885, which heretofore had been solely orchestral. Dankmar Adler, on account of his success in designing Central Music Hall, was called in to transform the northern end of the Exposition Building into a vast auditorium for the presentation of opera. In the March number, 1885, of the *Inland Architect*, that splendid magazine which did so much for the architecture and architects of Chicago in the eighties and nineties, is a double-page pen and ink drawing exquisitely done by Paul Lauthrop (a famous Scandinavian draughtsman whom the old timers will remember) of the interior of the Exposition Building as remodeled by Adler and Sullivan. It obviously was designed by Sullivan ornamentally, but the receding arches, the funnel-like shape, the pitch of the floors, etc., all of which resulted in well nigh perfect acoustics, were the work of Adler. To show that there was nothing small in the vision of public-spirited citizens or in their architects fifty years ago, this building within a building as reconstructed showed a stage eighty by one hundred twenty feet; the parquet seated 2238, behind and above, the dress circle seated 1486, the main balcony, 1834, and in addition there were boxes seating 300—altogether over 6000 people. It is a delight to record that the tremendous chance that a handful of courageous men took to introduce opera on a grand scale was a brilliant success and left them with a substantial fund. $132,000 was taken in for fourteen performances, at that time a world record. The names of some of these magnificent gamblers should be spread on this record. Ferdinand W. Peck was president, W. P. Nixon, vice-president. Among the directors appear the names of A. A. Sprague, Henry Field, John R. Walsh, R. T. Crane, George F. Harding, Louis Wahl, and N. K. Fairbank was doubtless somewhere in the picture.

So when the Auditorium came into the office of Adler and Sullivan in the summer of 1886 it most certainly was Adler's job particularly, as he was chosen without competition, with every architect in town after the commission.

A more difficult or complicated problem could hardly be presented to an architect. Under one roof were to be included a hotel, an office building and a huge auditorium, each to be a step ahead of the very latest and best.

The planning of a tri-partite building of this sort and on so grand a scale presented serious problems, to which were added engineering difficulties peculiar to a muddy clay soil which offered no firm bearing for foundations short of seventy feet below the surface. Caissons, solid columns of concrete down to bed rock, had not been invented, neither had skeleton construction which would have greatly lightened the load and simplified the construction. The highly perfected sciences of ventilation and air conditioning were in their infancy, and in the cradle with them was electric lighting and the use of electricity for power. Adler had no wealth of scientific information in regard to stage equipment and operation such as is at our elbow today. Nor was there any precedent in America for the vast stage and auditorium that he was bidden to create. He did go to Europe visiting theaters, but certain technical drawings that he had made there had to be re-designed to fit our local conditions. Sullivan said,[8] "The problems that Mr. Adler had to meet in that building were simply heart breaking. In those days there were very few consulting engineers."

So Adler, the engineer who designed Sherman's bridges in his march to the sea, applied his practical genius to solving the interminable problems that arose at every turn in the building of the Auditorium. The solution most talked about in his day was that applied to the foundations of the great tower. As all foundations had to be figured to settle uniformly in so spongy a soil, it occurred to Adler that the great foundations of the tower would

[8] Morrison, *op. cit.,* p. 108.

not settle their full quota until all the weight was applied to them, which meant not until the tower was completed, whereas, the hotel and office buildings, much lower on either side, would settle much more rapidly.

This unequal settlement would certainly cause a crack or rupture along the line where the building joined the tower. Adler's answer to this brain twister and sleep destroyer was to load artificially the floor of the tower, as the building ascended, with sand and lead so that the load per square foot on the foundations of the tower was always the same as that on the foundations on either side. As his tower passed the tenth story, the height of the adjoining parts, he began to unload so that at the time they were putting the cap stones on the finished tower they were wheeling the last load of sand and lead out of the front door! However, the problem of settling wasn't finally licked until 1893, when caissons or pillars of concrete down to bed rock were devised (on one of Adler's buildings by the way).

In those days statistics of big things fed people's imaginations and tickled their pride. Today they bore us. How many times around the world the strands of the Atlantic Cable would stretch for instance. Perhaps we ought to give a few sensible ones on the Auditorium. Its cost was $3,145,291, which was about thirty-six cents a cubic foot [9]—of interest to architects who have to struggle with costs from a dollar to a dollar and a half per cubic foot for an office building—and at that it was by far the most expensive building per foot that had ever been built in Chicago, and it took three years to build. The auditorium proper is the most interesting, famous and beautiful part of the whole. Curiously, it doesn't touch the street at any part, but is like an oyster inclosed in its shell, one valve

[9] Morrison, *op. cit.*

of which is the hotel and the other the office building. The theater seated 4237. Before it was remodeled some years ago the orchestra circle and the parquet extended in one tremendous sweep back to the foyer. The introduction of additional boxes, which completed the continuity of the "diamond horseshoe," has taken away some of the breath-taking qualities of the vast room but has made it more intimate. Holabird and Root in 1932 renovated the interior and restored the color scheme of Sullivan, blotting out the tomato red of an amateur decorator. But we were considering statistics. The stage is ninety-eight feet in the clear from side to side and sixty-two from front to back. I can vouch for this, for we had an intimate tennis club which, between opera seasons and after dinner at the Cliff Dwellers, played on a full size double court laid out on the stage of the Auditorium. Some of those in that far-off happy day were Guy Hardy, assistant manager of the opera, Bert Leston Taylor (B.L.T.), Percy Hammond, dramatic critic of the *Tribune,* Karleton Hackett, music critic of the *Post,* Henry Kitchell Webster, novelist, Will Carlton, librarian.

But we are constantly being weaned away from our statistics. Let us have some from *Industrial Chicago* published only a year or so after the completion of the building. "The Auditorium has a frontage of 362 feet on Congress Street, 187½ on Michigan Boulevard, and 162 on Wabash Avenue. Maine granite and buff Bedford stone form the exterior of the walls. Seventeen million bricks were used in the interior walls, and 6,000 tons of iron and steel in the whole building. Sixty thousand square feet of polished plate glass, or 50,000,000 pieces, marble of Italian mosaic in the floors; 30,000 square feet of French mosaics, and 60,000 square feet of ornamental tile. There are 500 windows, 2,000 doors, 10,000 electric lights, 11 dynamos, 230 miles of electric wire and cable, ... 25 miles of gas and water pipes, 11 boilers, 21 pumping engines, and 13 elevators. No less than 25,500 pounds of white lead and 46,875 square feet of gold leaf were used in the decorations."

No wonder we were proud! And now fifty years later, forgetting how many million bricks and how many miles of wire but realizing what the Auditorium meant in the upbuilding of Chicago and what it meant to the future of architecture in America, we are prouder still. We should preserve our "Palazzo Vecchio" forever.

THE BOARD OF TRADE. In Harriet Monroe's life of her brother-in-law, John Root, she tells the little known story of a competition for the Board of Trade—certainly not as famous but about as painful as that for the City Hall and County Building. This occurred during the winter of 1881; a building committee of five was selected not, as Miss Monroe says, for their qualifications, but because they had the leisure to serve. A general competition was ordered and five Chicago firms were invited to submit plans at a fee of one thousand dollars each. Burnham and Root submitted three schemes. One of these received popular acclaim but the committee was fearful of its originality and ordered another contest based, according to Miss Monroe, on one of the schemes suggested by Burnham and Root—a strange proceeding. In their second scheme John Donaghue, brilliant and tragic sculptor, designed the sculptural decoration, "showing Chicago, crowned with elevators, whose form became decorative as battlements, receiving the products of the world." A bitter wrangle ensued in the committee, which finally voted to accept "a hocus-pocus sort of whispering-gallery affair . . . . designed by a local creator of abominations." Whereupon a petition was circulated among the members of the board against accepting the "absurd design." The committee, bewildered by the complicated situation, compromised on the design of Boyington, which was finally erected. Burnham and Root's designs, which came so close to being chosen, were burned in the destruction of the Grannis Block. Burnham said it was one of the most brilliant conceptions of his gifted partner. We would give a good deal to see it, as it came at the critical moment when architecture was swiftly turning from the Parvenu to the Romantic.

William W. Boyington, when he won this competition, was sixty-three, which makes old timers of most of us I suppose, but shouldn't. We don't know what he thought of Richardson's Trinity Church, but he must have felt the thunder below, for the Montauk, Pullman, Calumet, Counselman, etc., were either on the boards or in the air, when in December, 1882, the corner-stone was laid. These all indicated, as we know, a new expression in architecture and, particularizing, they were all more or less in the Romanesque style. They were most certainly not in the old fashioned Parvenu garb of the seventies, which Boyington elected to use. By 1885, when the Board of Trade was opened, a great many of the great Romanesque office buildings had been built and Chicago's first "skeleton skyscraper" was a year old. Hence, the Board of Trade, like the City Hall and Court House, was outmoded and old-fashioned by the time it was completed. It occupied the site of the present building, built in 1926, perhaps the noblest site in Chicago, at the head of La Salle Street. It fronted one hundred seventy-three feet on Jackson and had a tower three hundred feet high. This tower had settled so seriously that about ten years after it was built it was taken down to the roof level.

Going back to the question of style, which seems to

agitate this author so much—we have in this great building (described as "the most elaborate and expensive in
the world"),[10] not only all the highness and narrowness
but the "Eastlake" chamfers, incised ornament, mansard
roofs and bedstead motives that we would expect in a
building of the early seventies. The tower at the roof level
changes to Victorian Gothic, and one commentator refers
to the building as being in "American Gothic Style."
Today we would have irreverently said that it had everything on but the kitchen stove. Give it a good mark,
however, for its huge trading room one hundred fifty-two
by one hundred sixty-one feet and eighty feet high.
Truthfully expressed in the exterior, and abiding in
memory's eye as full of color from the stained glass
windows; with many marble mosaics and frescoes and
mahogany; full of motion from the frantic traders; full
of noise as wheat, corn, hogs and lard varied a point
or two, and full of tobacco smoke whose blue haze, pierced
by the shafts of sunlight through the lofty windows, gave
an eerie splendor to the scene.

THE CHICAGO CLUB. We used to say that next to the
Field Wholesale by Richardson the best piece of architecture in the city was the Chicago Club by Burnham and
Root. Probably incorrect, but this handsome Romanesque
building on the southwest corner of Van Buren and Michigan was the gem of the Avenue from the time of its
completion in 1882, as the Art Institute, to its accidental
collapse while being remodelled in 1929. The Chicago
Club seemed to be a sponsor of good architecture for it
built and occupied for many years the handsome Victorian
Gothic building on Monroe opposite the Palmer House
and now demolished. This they abandoned to De Jonghe's
and his snails Bourgogne for the vacated Art Institute

[10] *Industrial Chicago.*

at the southwest corner of Michigan and Van Buren. This famous building was more orthodox in its Romanesque treatment than any other that Root had designed. Undoubtedly he felt his responsibility as the designer of the vessel which would contain the treasures of ancient as well as of modern art. The façade of only four stories and attic was notable for the strong arched portal that Root always thought essential, for its *piano nobile* of mighty arches, three across the front, four on the side, and for its great dominating gable richly decorated with carving at its apex. Again the architect praises the "scale"—a word which must annoy the layman no end. It is not mere jargon. It signifies the mutual relationship in size between the different parts of a building and of the ornament to them. For instance, in this case the ornament is unusually broad and strong, just the right size and just the right depth to harmonize with the structure of the building and to bring out its maximum nobility and beauty.

MARSHALL FIELD WHOLESALE.   Out at the Lake Zurich Golf Club, an oasis for some of us in this desert of modernity, is a wide bench under a great oak tree outlooking to a lovely view of hill and dale. Parenthetically, it was set up in memory of Horace Oakley. The thick oak seat is laid on two pilaster capitals strongly sculptured in red sandstone, as crisp and fresh as when they came from the chisel of the carver fifty-four years ago. As far as I know these are the sole remains of the famous Field Wholesale Building, destroyed in 1930—the masterpiece of H. H. Richardson, acclaimed from the day of its completion to the day of its destruction as Chicago's noblest work of architecture. Perhaps one shouldn't expect a great corporation to carry a building that is unsound or unprofitable for sentimental reasons. But this building was as strong as a cliff of granite, and it is unbelievable

MARSHALL FIELD WHOLESALE, 1885, H. H. RICHARDSON, ARCHITECT

Formerly at Adams, Quincy, Wells, and Franklin streets

that no use could have been found for it. At least it should
have been given a reprieve of a year or two to find its
place again. However, with a singular lack of imagination,
to say nothing of reverence, the great firm which built
it destroyed it without a qualm. Perhaps if the public and
the architects had shown the slightest interest it might
have been saved. This author raised his feeble voice in
protest in a letter to one of our great newspapers which
advertises itself as "undominated," but for some reason
or other the letter never appeared. However, Chicago's
masterpiece of its most vigorous days is gone; and there
is little use crying over spilt genius.

It occupied the entire block between Adams, Quincy,
Wells and Franklin. Richardson died in April, 1886, so he
did not live to see the completion of his great work, notwithstanding his prayer on his death-bed that he live two
years to see the completion of the Pittsburgh Jail and of
the Field Wholesale. Constructionally, the building was
of reddish granite, Richardson's favorite material, in the
lower stories and red sandstone above. The color of the
two varied but harmonized beautifully. The granite was
rock face, the sandstone tooled. The interior was of "mill"
or slow burning construction. It was seven stories high.
It cost $800,000. The building measured three hundred
twenty-five feet by one hundred ninety and one hundred
twenty feet high—a vast stone chest sheltering, along with
the bales of merchandise, the light and the way to a
greater architecture.

Architecturally, the style is Romanesque and in accordance with the invariable wish of Marshall Field there
was little ornament, the only sculptured portions being
the pilaster caps mentioned above. It combined power
and grace to a sensational degree—power in the cyclopean
size of the granite blocks and the huge span of the first

story arches, grace in the subtlety of the proportions. The façade was slightly divided into base shaft and cap like this, 1-3-2-1, in which one story occupied the powerful battered base—five stories of the shaft were confined in two arcades, the lower containing three stories and the upper two—while the frieze, the seventh story, was an almost continuous series of narrow windows. The building was crowned by a strong but slightly projecting cornice of unusual design. Although Chicago architects were active partisans and resented the intrusion of foreigners—witness their glee over the tribulations of Mullen the government architect—yet they acclaimed the Field Wholesale as a masterpiece and accepted it as a model.

Louis Sullivan in his weariness in journeying through the desert (as he considered it) of American contemporary architecture found refreshment and rest in the oasis of Richardson's Field Wholesale. In the chapter of his *Kindergarten Chats* called the "Oasis" he has many things to say of it. "Here," he says, "is a man for you to look at. A man . . . . that has active muscles, heart, lungs, viscera; a man that lives and breathes, that has red blood; a real man; a manly man; a virile force, broad, vigorous, energetic; spiritually an entire male. . . . . Four square and brown, it stands, in physical fact, a monument to trade, to the organized commercial spirit, to the power and progress of the age, to the strength and resource of individuality and force of character; it stands as the index of a mind large enough, courageous enough to cope with these things, master them, absorb them and give them forth impressed with the stamp of larger and forceful personality; artistically, it stands as the oration of one who knows well how to choose his words, who has somewhat to say and says it—and says it as the outpouring of a copious, direct, large and simple mind."

John Root was equally appreciative and equally indebted. One gathers that the Chicago architects welcomed such an outstanding work by Richardson as a convenient norm and model. Certainly the Romanesque took great strides forward on its completion.

CHURCH ARCHITECTURE

In no department of architecture was the Romantic movement more ruthless in its destruction of old ideals than in church building. There is little use in describing again the high narrow angular Victorian Gothic church of the sixties and seventies, built almost invariably of rough face Joliet stone or, lacking that, of Milwaukee brick. The motive was the high and narrow, and the façade with its light thin gable was dominated by a higher thinner spire. The Sunday school, usually of one big room, was in the basement. The auditorium was above, often with an encircling gallery. The windows were high and narrow, filled with simple stained glass in diamond panes. The woodwork, especially the pews, was walnut if possible. The wood carving was incised or jig sawed, and the painted ornament was a feeble Gothic stencil, usually in brick red.

The change about 1880 was complete and in toto—in style, in material, in arrangement—and while one can scarcely claim this revolution extended to religion it did at least encompass the teaching of the Sunday school.

The change in style was from Victorian Gothic to Richardsonian Romanesque, and this was more complete than in any other type of building. Seldom, if ever, did Queen Anne, who battled the Romanesque to a draw in domestic architecture, even venture to enter the ring.

The change of material was from Joliet limestone, the

old "Athens marble" of Van Osdel's days, to Bedford stone.

These two stones most popular in the Chicago area are very different in character. We have already described the white, almost chalky, limestone from the Joliet and Lemont quarries, almost impossible to carve and maintaining its yellow whiteness in a mysterious fashion against all the assaults of soot and weather that Chicago can bring to bear.

Bedford stone is a creamy grey or a bluish grey limestone made from the age-long deposit of minute crustaceans. It comes, as everyone knows, from the great quarries of southern Indiana. It is a magnificent stone to carve but dirt sticks to it like a poor relation, and it was used rock face like the Joliet stone. Two other materials rushed to the front to discredit the Gothic churches. One was red pressed brick, often known as Anderson press brick. The other was terra cotta made at first about the same color as the brick. These later were used usually in combination.

As startling as the changes in style and material was the metamorphosis that overwhelmed the plan. In the first place the Sunday school was dragged out of the ground and set up in the light. This was largely owing to Bishop Vincent's revolutionary crusade for the neglected Sunday school and his invention of the Akron Plan, so called from its demonstration in the Methodist Church in Akron, Ohio. The bishop's shibboleth was "Togetherness and Separateness." In this new idea the Sunday school of all ages gathered in one big squarish room, lighted usually by a skylight, for the opening exercises—the Togetherness. At the signal they slipped in squads of ten or twelve for study into small class rooms which formed the sides of the assembly room, usually in two stories, separated from the big room by folding doors or curtains—the Separateness. For the closing exercises the operation was reversed or the classes could even remain in their cubicals and take part in the general exercises. Sometimes the Sunday school could be opened up completely into the church by the disappearance on rollers of the partition that separated the two. In passing it may be said that the Akron Plan was abandoned about 1910 for the departmental Sunday school and the parish house.

The auditorium itself followed the example of its swan mother, Trinity in Boston. It was square rather than long. Sometimes the floors were bowled or sloped. It was a "color" church with hand painted decorations on walls and ceiling and a peacock's tail of organ pipes. Some were so "modern" that the pulpit and choir were tucked into a corner and "opera chairs" were used instead of pews. The wood was "golden oak." A tremendous change occurred in the glass. A Romanesque interior called for a few very large windows instead of the many narrow ones in a Gothic fane. This meant a "Tiffany window," if the congregation could possibly afford it. "Tiffany windows" depicted biblical scenes in a realistic manner, but unless they were by the master, they were apt to be of doubtful artistic value. Now, acknowledging defeat, we have gone back to Chartres. In the church of today, with the lengthened nave and open chancel and its twelfth century glass not a single feature introduced by those churches of the eighties that were so very, very modern has survived. Many of the present-day churches are splendid examples of church architecture, but it must be admitted that except in the upper brackets the Romanesque Revival Churches committed as many architectural sins as the Victorian Gothic that they derided and supplanted.

DOMESTIC ARCHITECTURE

It cannot be said that Chicago's contribution to domestic architecture in the Romantic Age was notable. It was enthusiastic, exuberant, imaginative perhaps, but distinguished or influential it was not; not comparable certainly to her eminent contribution to the art and science of the high building. Nevertheless the revolution in design of the home from the seventies to the eighties was just as profound. However, the models for this revolution were not indigenous; they were found in the Eastern States. Chicago's contribution, such as it was, lay in the testing of a greater variety of plans and of exteriors and particularly of materials and practical devices. As John Root writes in his enthusiasm, "Not a day passes but specimens are brought of new materials, granite from Wisconsin, sand-stones from Michigan, onyx from Mexico, marbles from Colorado to California. There is an equally steady current of new processes for art-metal work in bronze and iron, of mosaics in glass and marble, of rich wall coverings in leather, stuffs, and even stamped wood-pulp and in new forms of beautiful encaustic materials. With a wholesome quality of mind and life in the layman and with imagination and discrimination in the architect, what may not our domestic architecture become? In twenty years this will be the richest and most luxurious country ever known upon the globe." [11]

The parvenu taste of the sixties and seventies, including the rebuilding of Chicago after the Fire, left little of inspiration for the lusty young modernists of the eighties.

[11] Posthumous article by John Root in *Homes in City and County,* 1892.

The "Athens marble" façades with their galvanized iron cornices all glorifying the high and narrow ideal and particularly the cramped plans with the narrow hall-ways and high stoops, after the New York fashion, left little to inspire and nothing to emulate. Inevitably, and we trust unconsciously, our young men looked to their more experienced brothers in the East. At the Centennial Exposition of 1876, which created so much amusement to a later generation, there was a group of English half-timbered cottages which served as the headquarters of the English Commission. They were simple, frank and in good taste. According to Bruce Price, distinguished New York architect of long ago, these awakened great interest and excited a beneficent unrest on architect and layman alike.[12] At any rate shortly after in the East the minds of architect and public were opened wide to English influence, and this was the advent of the celebrated Queen Anne style of the late seventies and eighties.

This author is conscious that he is often prone to crowd fads and fancies into architectural pigeon holes which they ill fit. Yet after all a thing hardly exists as a fact unless it is given a name and certainly without a name it is hardly describable.

The Queen Anne in England and the Romanesque as revived in America were styles originally conceived to be executed in masonry, and when seen in masonry are easily recognized, but what of the vaster number of buildings, mostly houses, which had to be built of America's most convenient material—wood?

In the East, to which our young architects looked, some extremely interesting houses were built which were true and original expressions of their material—wood—and

[12] Chapter in *Homes in City and Country*, 1892.

which had beauty and repose as well. Through at least
two generations these have not been out-moded—the best
of all tests. Richardson did two notable ones, one for
Mrs. M. F. Stoughton in Cambridge, in 1882 and another
for Dr. Walter Channing in Brookline. Both of these were
all of shingles with scarcely any ornament, though picturesque (the most favored of adjectives in those days)
in mass. They could scarcely be called Romanesque nor
can they be yclept Queen Anne with any justice. Charles
F. McKim, who never more than flirted with the Queen
Anne nor the Romanesque, in the late seventies built
several low-lying houses in shingles and siding, which
owed more to our New England Colonial than to any
imported style, and W. R. Emerson did the like about
Boston and Bar Harbour; so did Arthur Little and Bruce
Price.

If you turn to the *American Architect* of 1877 you
will find along the middle of the volume a house in New
Brighton, Staten Island, built for A. J. Hamilton, also a
gardener's cottage and stable for Mr. William Krebs, both
by Mr. Bassett Jones. These buildings are undoubtedly
the ones referred to by Bruce Price when he says, "Mr.
Bassett Jones, fresh from the studio and influence of Norman Shaw, has built one or two lovely cottages on Staten
Island." The *American Architect* refers to them "as
somewhat free adaptation of Queen Anne forms." To this
searcher they are the first examples of the Queen Anne
mode in the United States. The style caught on at once
and spread like wild fire and the *American Architect*
which in its first issues of 1877 is almost exclusively filled
with houses in the Victorian Gothic mode, all high and
narrow and jig sawed, is in its later issues replete with
sketches for houses mostly all shingled, with lower roofs,
lower and broader windows and turned, instead of jig

sawed, columns and ornaments. The plans underwent a sea change too. Halls became suddenly wide and square and contained fireplaces, a new idea, and porches were greatly widened and lengthened, often turning the corner and obscuring the sunlight of all the windows of the front room. These very early Queen Anne houses in the East were really the best of the lot. Unhappily, as the style moved west the simplicity and taste of the earliest examples were swallowed up into exuberant vagaries and experiments. But before it is too late, how came and what is the Queen Anne Style? There have been several accounts of the origin of "Queen Anne." I was surprised to find one of the best in *Industrial Chicago,* published in 1891. It has the advantage anyway of being nearer to the scene. It relates how Norman Shaw, the English architect, in 1863 was called upon to make alterations in Cranbrook Hall built in Queen Anne's reign (1702-14). This was an austere box-like structure and Shaw, being young, lively, and inventive, rejuvenated the old timer with bay windows and other architectural beauty-aids with great success, so that Nesfield, another brilliant member of the influential coterie to which Shaw belonged, referred to this success as being in Shaw's "Queen Anne Style." Most accounts date the mode from the building of New Zealand Chambers in Leadenhall Street, London in 1873. At any rate, in a nutshell, what had happened was this. The younger school of English architects was thoroughly tired of the Gothic Revival. Shaw's experiments in what he called "Free Classic" gave the clue. The architecture of Queen Anne, the first quarter of the 18th century and contemporary with Sir Christopher Wren, was the freest of English Classic styles and, like its imitator of one hundred seventy-five years later, an architecture primarily of brick. With it as a basis every sort of liberty and variation was allowed and encouraged. There are countless examples in England but very few of them are of wood. There as here, the theme song was romance and freedom.

So there were two pathways from the east, one emanating from the Romanesque Revival and the other from the Queen Anne importation, and they came together in the wooden house. For the wooden house, the Queen Anne style with its vagaries and license was an answer to prayer. This to the Romanesque was certainly a hard nut to crack. For one reason masonry is of the essence in the Romanesque. There was no precedent and no place, it seemed, for anything as ephemeral as wood. The arch, for instance, is the sign manual of the Romanesque but is always an anomaly in wood, and so are deep reveals. About the only features that could be translated was the ornament, which with certain modifications could be carved in wood or cast in plaster. There was also the indefinable glamour that Richardson put into the Romanesque in color and variety of material that the wooden house made valiant attempts to appropriate.

I remember a house being built when I was a small boy in Evanston for Dr. Charles G. Fuller. The architects were Burnham and Root. The Fuller house was similar in treatment to Richardson's Stoughten house in Cambridge, built in 1882, or to the Channing house. In both of these the round arches and the characteristic ornament of the Romanesque were followed where possible and the stone texture was imitated, or at least symbolized by shingled walls, but this unobtrusive type, excellent as it was, appealed only to the intelligentsia. These rare houses, while picturesque in mass, were simple in architectural treatment—the walls entirely of shingles stained, no cornice or projecting eaves—the chimneys broad and high—often the upper sash of the windows latticed—columns and spindles turned. The house called for a setting of trees. Perhaps this is the reason why the examples that I remember were in Evanston. It would readily become a sort of Colonial if a gambrel roof were employed and the detail took on a classic tinge, which is what Charles McKim did to it in his early days. This type, which certainly was not Queen Anne, probably was founded upon the Richardson examples and lasted well into and beyond the World's Fair period.

The decade from 1880 to 1890 was one of tremendous architectural growth for Chicago. Not only was the city to be rebuilt, but its limits were extended to include the city of Lake View and Jefferson, an area stretching from Fullerton to Devon and from the lake to Central. At the same time the city was extended south to include the village of Hyde Park and the town of Lake from 39th to the Indiana State line and west to 48th Avenue. The following year Washington Heights was added so that in the eighties Chicago was quadrupled in area. The architecture of all of this tremendous space is predominantly that of the period we are discussing. For instance there are large areas principally residential on the Northwest Side and in Hyde Park well built up where evidently there has scarcely been a new house built in the last forty-five years. Almost all of this architecture is of this incongruous wayward, even mongrel but highly romantic, type which we call "Queen Anne."

I have before me a rare volume—the *Inland Architect* of the years 1883-5, Volume II, I believe. This was the heyday of the Romanesque or Romantic revival and the pages of the *Inland Architect* with their zinc etchings and halftone or two, a process newly developed, are eloquent of the trend of the day. A tabulation of these buildings ought to furnish an indication of the stylistic trends of the eighties, though it is understood that a hard and fast classification is impossible, as not a few round arched (Romanesque) buildings have the wood turned grilles, etc., of the Queen Anne type and vice versa. Here they are for what they are worth.

In the Romanesque style there were six houses, six public buildings and seventeen commercial buildings. Of the "Queen Anne" style twenty houses and four public buildings were illustrated. Of hold-overs from the previous Parvenu age there were six of various types, of French Renaissance one, of Elizabethan three, of Moorish (popular for interiors) three and only one pure enough to be termed Classic, and but one Gothic church. It should be remembered, however, that the great majority of the buildings of this day were houses too humble or too ugly to be reproduced. These for the great part were Queen Anne in some mongrel variation of the style.

John Root's enthusiastic statement about new materials and new processes is fully borne out in the hosts of new materials made available for building the house. The advance in heating, plumbing and lighting was as sudden and as extensive. A contemporary comments on a wave of remodeling that set in with the eighties—the removal of small windows to give place to large ones, especially to single panes of heavy glass, shingling all over, etc., etc. Perhaps the wealth of new materials, the prosperity of city and nation, the exuberance of full steam, are sufficient reasons for the popularity of the Queen Anne style in our domestic architecture, but I'm afraid not. The compelling reason after all was fashion. The mode in England, the accepted manner in Boston, the *dernier cri* in New York—why should Chicago lag behind? Of the countless examples of Queen Anne there is none better

THE CHARLES B. FARWELL HOUSE, TREAT AND FOLTZ, ARCHITECTS, BUILT IN 1882

than the Charles B. Farwell (Senator) on Pearson Street, just west of the Drive. That of his brother John V. Farwell was next door on the corner. These two houses were "projected" in 1882 and each cost over $100,000.[13]

The architects of the Charles Farwell house were Treat and Foltz. This house has all the characteristics of the real Queen Anne—Classic detail used in an unorthodox but not in a debased way. Note the entrance columns, the high roof and elaborate chimneys and particularly the very steep pediments, especially characteristic, as is also the all over red color scheme, brick and sandstone in this case. His brother's house, destroyed in the widening of Michigan Avenue, was decidedly of the Romanesque persuasion, at least it was rock faced stone and it had a corner tower with a dome-like roof—always a popular feature in the Romanesque house. One is a little surprised at finding it damned by Burnham and Root, but perhaps the detail redeemed the "just so and so" appearance of the house.

The interior of the Charles B. Farwell house, as illustrated in the *Inland Architect,* was typical of the mansions of the eighties. The great entrance hall aspired to the ideal of a baronial manor house with panelled wainscot (of golden oak), an enormous fireplace niche (with a microscopic grate opening), a beamed ceiling, walls and ceilings covered with stenciled canvas, and here and there crossed scimitars, bronze statues, brass plaques, antlers, inlaid tables, Jacobean furniture and two early American Windsor chairs looking very self-concious and out of place. From the ceiling hung two enormous oriental lamps of elaborate wrought metal. You may walk in it today, fifty-five years later, and have the thrill of comparing it with the photograph. It is just the same, minus the furni-

[13] *Industrial Chicago,* I, 260.

ture and the lamps and the peace and plenty of the romantic eighties.

The still younger men, disciples of Richardson, like Root, made lots of fun of the contemporary Queen Anne. However, it had its apologists. Professor Ricker of "Champaign Illinois University" wrote: "Our Queen Anne style certainly contains many false quantities in architectural grammar, many vulgarities, but it is our own, not really an imitation of the English Queen Anne. It is adapted to its uses and is a flexible and living style capable of new combinations." [14] In the same article he also wrote: "Norman Shaw introduced the present Queen Anne Style, it being first an imitation of an earlier English style, though soon greatly modified and improved, especially in this country. It was at first derided by the profession, but in spite of ridicule it has almost supplanted other styles in the English-speaking world."

GLESSNER HOUSE. In the early part of 1936 Emory Hall, Arthur Woltersdorf and I were received by Mrs. Lee, daughter of J. J. Glessner, in the famous old house on Prairie Avenue. We were there because Mr. Glessner had, through the efforts of Alfred Granger, bequeathed the house to the Chicago Chapter of the American Institute of Architects on condition that they carry out certain provisos of his. Most unfortunately they were unable or, more accurately, unwilling to exercise their option, so the house reverted to the estate. Our job was to estimate the minimum changes which would be required to make it suitable for occupancy by the architects. That story is too long, complicated and unhappy. I'll make no attempt to recount it here, but the reminiscences of Mrs. Lee were very interesting. She said that the commission for the house was won by Richardson in competition with

[14] *Inland Architect,* November, 1885.

W. A. Potter of New York. Richardson apparently before the competition visited Mr. Glessner and in his presence made a sketch of the ground plan, which was substantially as built. The house was commissioned May, 1885, and took a year to build, which meant that Richardson was to die before its completion. It was completed along with the Field Wholesale and MacVeagh house by Shepley, Rutan and Coolidge, the famous firm organized to complete Richardson's work. The house when we saw it had scarcely been changed from its original conditions. William Prettyman, the decorator, did the parlor walls. The great library table and the dining room chairs were designed by Richardson. The rugs in the library and in first and second stair halls were designed by William Morris. With the exception of one lavatory, all the plumbing and fixtures were original, and the exposed plumbing pipes were something new in 1886. Needless to say the great house reeked with human and artistic interest. The walls were covered with autographed photographs of the famous musicians, Schumann Heink and Paderewski. Stories of Marshall Field walking to town trailed by his carriage with its liveried footmen, of George M. Pullman from across the street, of poker games at Norman Ream's, etc., etc., while not of the essence, detracted nothing from the atmosphere of the grand old place. It is pleasant to relate that the great bones of the Glessner house are safe from molestation. For, following the inability of the Architects to accept the gift, the house has been acquired by the Armour Institute of Technology.

Few of the post-war generation have any idea of the size and sumptuousness of the great houses of the eighties. It is a commentary on the new puritanism or the new poverty that the erection of any one of these would be almost unthinkable today. Let him go to the Burnham

Library of the Art Institute and turn the plates of "Artistic Houses" published in 1883-84 (and by the way the volume belonged to Marshall Field), and he will get an idea of how the very rich were housed in the Romantic Age.

POTTER PALMER HOME. By far the most famous, probably the largest, and by all odds the most imposing house in our city is the Potter Palmer mansion, a mansion to end all mansions, which at this writing it seems to have done. It stands, as everyone knows, on Lake Shore Drive between Banks and Schiller. As architectural fashions have flowed and ebbed it has been admired and derided, along with its more venerable neighbor the water tower, but no citizen in Chicago or lover of her traditions or her beauty could see the towers of this castle over-thrown without real sorrow.

Built in 1882 it came very early in the Romanesque Queen Anne regime. As a matter of fact it has nothing to do with either. It's an American architect's best thought of what a baronial castle should be. Early photographs and illustrations in the periodicals of the time show a building not nearly as pleasing as the castle we see today. The lighter limestone trim, finished smooth against the rough faced brown stone made a startling and agitating pattern. Now the kindly patina of smoke and weather have toned it down to a uniform hue.

If you must have the style, it is Gothic—English of the latter square headed variety. The interior indulged in the luxurious eclecticism of the time. Sheldon's artistic *Country Seats* gives a description of Mrs. Palmer's bedroom. "All the woodwork of this sumptuous apartment is in ebony and gold. The wall spaces are painted in oil after Moorish designs. The ceiling is carved and entirely of wood; the windows are like those in the palace at Cairo, being entirely of lattice work. At the top of the windows is a Moorish arch of ebony, and in the arch cathedral glass in different shades of orange and lemon. The settees and chairs are covered with Smyrna rugs; the paneled wainscot is of wood cut into geometrical designs and the chandeliers to match are of gold and garnet glass." The general result is an "Oriental dream." These decorations were done by Mr. R. W. Bates of Chicago. Messrs. Herter of New York did the hall and the dining-room. This book tells how the great Richardson visited the house and pronounced the mosaic floor in the hall, "the handsomest in the country." He also "spoke warmly in praise of the woodwork, the carvings and the glass-enameled Venetian mosaic of the walls."

THE INVENTION OF SKELETON
CONSTRUCTION

In 1884 a typical elevator building was ten stories high. The interior was constructed of cast-iron columns with wrought-iron girders and beams, which in turn supported primitive fireproof floors composed of brick or tile arches. All of the exterior walls were of solid masonry strong enough to support not only themselves but their share of the floor loads. Thus the building reached upwards keeping step with the rapidly improving safety and speed of the passenger elevator. The walls, as necessary, became thicker at an average rate of about four inches to a story. Any architect could foresee the limit. Even with a ten-story building the brick piers at the first floor would be four feet thick from front to back, yet the dancing elevator like a will-o-the-wisp beckoned them to fifteen and twenty stories. But how could this be done? The first story, let for shops, required the most light, but here most unfortunately the walls or piers must be the thickest and the widest. Even a wall four feet thick seriously cut off the light and, almost as bad, reduced the rentable area where it was the most valuable. The men of the eighties, like the dying Goethe, called for "light, more light." In the Pullman and Rookery buildings round granite shafts far stronger than brick or stone were substituted, which helped a little, but it makes little difference with the light whether this glass is placed at front or back.

Another serious difficulty was the enormous weight of the mighty walls and piers, which in time called for greater and heavier foundations. The clay and mud of Chicago's sub-soil were a headache to the architect when he had only a five story building, but they became vastly more painful when the building was doubled in height. We saw how John Root helped out at this point with his raft or floating foundation of railroad iron and concrete but the limit here could easily be foreseen, with buildings steadily mounting higher and their weights steadily increasing. Was it the insistent demand of business for buildings big enough, which meant high enough, to house their pyramiding requirements? Was it the demand of the building investor for a building which would pay a return on property in the business district? Was it a megalomania of Chicago's architects desirous of astonishing the world and particularly New York? Or was it an inevitable accident that produced skeleton construction and the skyscraper? I think it was the last. I can find no record of any demand on an architect in Chicago for any building higher than the seventeen-story Monadnock, which was certainly over the practical limit for an elevator building. However, the architects may have felt that the owners seemed to be well satisfied with the ten-story heights of the elevator buildings.

There was one thing that the owner could always safely demand and that was light. This was especially true in our big square downtown blocks where it was often very difficult to plan the building without deep offices. Hence a very important renting point was light offices. At least two Chicago firms specialized in big window openings and glass areas. One was Adler and Sullivan, and the other William Le Baron Jenney. Adler and Sullivan in the Troescher Building trembled on the edge of the discovery but it was Jenney who stumbled upon it in his Home Insurance Building. The great discovery is of course skeleton construction. As we have dealt so much in definitions—what is skeleton construction? In skeleton construction a steel skeleton or cage consisting of columns, girders and beams is first erected and on this skeleton is hung all the rest of the building, consisting of exterior walls, floors, partitions and roof, thereby, upsetting the five thousand year custom of supporting the building on enclosing walls of frame or masonry.

Major Jenney had a particular zest for getting in his buildings as much light as possible. It is quite likely that, being a good business man, he wanted to make his unusually light offices a "selling point" for his firm. The best way to get the most light, other things being equal, was to get the biggest windows possible, and one way to get big windows was to cut down the size of the masonry piers. A very interesting experiment in that line was made by the Major in the building at the northwest corner of Wells and Monroe streets once called the "Leiter Building." This building is of "mill construction," that is, while the outside walls are of masonry the interior construction is of heavy wood girders, beams and posts. Instead of the ends of the girders resting on the outside walls Jenney put heavy posts against the inside of the exterior brick piers and rested his girders on these, thereby taking the load of the floors off the outside brick piers. Their job was thus reduced to enclosing the building and supporting nothing but themselves. By this clever and, as far as I know, unprecedented device Jenney reduced his piers to a minimum and in this manner got more light. This was a very important step toward the undreamed-of goal of skeleton construction. It required one step more and Major Jenney, with his Home Insurance Building, was the one who took it.

Today skeleton construction has a highly developed and standardized technique. Columns are of heavy rolled H sections or of various sections riveted or welded together; spandrels extending between the exterior columns are of plate girders; the facing of walls and piers is supported by angle irons riveted to the columns. At the proper places gusset plates, diagonal braces, heavy girders and other means are used to brace the building against wind pressure. The floors are usually of some special type of reinforced concrete suspended between girders or beams running from column to column. All of the above is of steel with a tensile strength of 50,000 to 70,000 pounds to the square inch. Today, in Chicago, solid cylinders of concrete called caissons extend from the basement down through seventy feet or more of clay to bed rock, supporting the skeleton of steel, which in its turn supports all the rest of the building. When the Home Insurance was designed in 1883 the only structural metal available was cast iron for the columns and wrought iron for the beams. Fireproof floors were made either of brick or tile segmental arches leveled on top with concrete or of flat tile arches. The necessity of fireproofing the wrought or cast iron was thoroughly appreciated, and that was done with slabs of terra cotta tile. Three types of foundations were known to the architects of the eighties—(1) wooden piles; (2) stepped foundations of stone; (3) floating foundations composed of crossed horizontal iron rails incased in concrete.

The skyscrapers that followed the Home Insurance Building, 1884, until the end of the World's Fair, 1893, constitute an extremely interesting and homogeneous class. In the first place, they reflected the tremendous increase in value of downtown property, which by 1891 reached an average of $3,600,000 per acre for choice business property in the "Loop." Second, they show the progressive improvement of building-engineering and construction and the perfection of the skeleton steel frame. And third, they present a distinct bracket in architectural design in which the men of the eighties in presenting the steel skeleton to the world clothed it in a dress they thought appropriate and which came near to being indigenous. After the Fair men attempted to bind the Classic style to their will in applying it to steel construction, and it took nearly thirty years of failure to make them give up the attempt. It must be remembered that all of these giants were built in a period of romantic *élan*, almost all by young men, fired with a conviction that Chicago was the wonder-city of the world and bolstered up in the idea by the amazement of Europe and by the grudging admiration of New York. It was the building of these skyscrapers that made Chicago, a mere stripling in age and background, the prodigy of the new world and the chosen son for the great Columbian Exposition.

Let us discuss elsewhere the theory of skeleton construction and the priority of the Home Insurance and consider these buildings now merely as frontispieces. Remember, we are in the heart of what is so often called the Romanesque Revival, but which we find is quite as much "free Classic" or "Queen Anne."

This is how a special writer for the *Chicago Tribune's* Sunday edition of September 13, 1891, lists "Chicago's Big Buildings." It is, in fact, a list, of Chicago's first skeleton steel skyscrapers with two exceptions, following the epoch-making Home Insurance. First of all is the Home Insurance, built in 1884, with this interesting description by architect Jenney himself: "In 1884 the Home Insurance Company of New York built the first tall fireproof, finely finished office-building in Chicago. It demanded the maximum amount of light, reducing the piers and walls to dimensions that forced the architect to adopt a new method of construction which has since been generally adopted and is now known as the 'Chicago Construction.'" The next building mentioned is the Rookery, not a skyscraper; then the Tacoma, northeast corner of La Salle and Madison, Holabird and Roche architects; then the Chamber of Commerce and the Owings Building, now the Bedford, an elevator building whose days have been numbered. These last three buildings, the account says, "ushered in the era of buildings whose stories extended into the teens." Then it dramatically compares "two great buildings" on opposite corners of Dearborn and Jackson: "The Northern Hotel, with its rows of handsome bays, is a steel frame-work with a covering wall which is not expected to carry even its own weight, while the walls of the Monadnock Building are of solid masonry which give it a severely plain but massive appearance." Both of these buildings were planned by Burnham and Root. It then mentions "two great buildings in which sentiment is mixed with cold business policy," the Masonic Temple and the Woman's Temple. "Both are nearing completion," the *Tribune* says.

The Masonic Temple within the year has been torn down, having lived nearly half a century. The Woman's Temple was razed in 1926. The "fleche of gold bronze seventy feet in height surmounted by the beautiful form of a woman in the attitude of prayer," was never built. Both of these were by Burnham and Root. The next in line, the Unity Building on Dearborn, seventeen stories high, was promoted by John P. Altgeld. Clinton J. Warren, the architect, explained that it was built of cast-iron columns instead of steel because the factor of safety was eight to one. Next is the Manhattan Building, Jenney and Mundie architects. William B. Mundie told me that that was the first building in Chicago with party walls supported by the steel skeleton, in other words the first complete skeleton construction building. It was sixteen stories in its central portion, with nine-story wings which were carried on cantilevers. The Cook County Abstract and Trust Company Building, Henry Ives Cobb, architect, promised even before completion to be one of the finest in the city, sixteen stories, to cost $700,000. (This is the present Chicago Title and Trust Building on Washington Street.) The paper proceeds:

"The Ashland Block designed by D. H. Burnham—John Root had just expired—is one of the latest great office building projects. It will be sixteen stories high and stand on the corner of Clark and Randolph. The new Fair Building as completed in accordance with the present plans will be one of the greatest commercial structures in the world. It will be eighteen stories high. It has not been decided if it will be completed in that height before the close of the World's Fair. At present it will be built in a first section of eight stories." As a fitting climax comes the announcement that the Odd Fellows will build a thirty-four story structure 556 feet in height. The writer comments, "It is considered possible from an architectural standpoint but not probable from the financial point of view." It was never built.

As I write this in 1939 there has not been a skyscraper built in Chicago since the Field Building, forty-two stories high, was erected in 1932. Is it possible that the last has been built on the site of the first? The financial *débâcle* of 1929 was a veritable Fall of Rome for Chicago building, especially for the skyscraper. A white togaed Roman senator in the year 410 might well have shaken his head over the dearth of new forums or circuses, but if he had thought the depression was temporary and building would boom again when Alaric had withdrawn with his barbarians, he would have waited a thousand years to see his hopes confirmed. While no such gloomy forecast is made for the American city, still we have reshaped our version of the "city of tomorrow," which in 1926 we saw as a fantastic concentration of unbelievable skyscrapers, the lower portions of which were girdled by subways, highways and super highways, and the tops, a quarter mile or more above, with mooring masts and landing platforms. We hope now rather for some sort of centripetal explosion that will hurl the Loop into outlying districts, abolishing crowded areas and redeeming blighted ones—and that might seal the doom of the skyscraper. Even if this should happen, and anything can in a new era, and if the skyscraper should become a museum piece, it still would rank as a high-water mark in America's architecture and Chicago would still be lustrous with the honor of having given it birth.

"Scorn not the skyscraper! Old Icarus would not have looked more enviously at Lindbergh's silvery plane than would the builders of Amiens and Beauvais, could they stand on Fifth Avenue, and follow with astonished eyes

the ascending shafts of Rockefeller Center to a height
that makes their own towering cathedrals seem puny and
infantile. The skyscraper is far and away the most important architectural achievement of America, her great
gift to the art of building. In its train has come the most
brilliant era of structural engineering that the world has
ever known. From the bottom of the lowest caisson, where
one hundred feet below the surface the pneumatic drills
have ground to a level the bones of mother earth, to the
top of the highest pinnacle, where the staccato notes of
the steel riveter drown out the hum of aeroplanes, the
vast pile of the skyscraper is fraught with the best construction efforts of the American mind. The engineers,
civil, electrical, mechanical, sanitary, have vied with each
other in perfecting the application of their science, and
the same emulation has existed among the trades—the
masons, the carpenters, the plasterers, the glaziers, the
painters; the setters of marble, of ornamental iron, of
mosaic and back of them the manufacturers of brick; the
quarry men who hew the stone; the great mills that saw
the lumber and fabricate the cabinet work; the kilns
that bake the terra cotta; the furnaces that roll the steel.
These with a myriad others form a vast army whose labors
now constitute, next to agriculture, our greatest industry
—an army that builds and destroys not, an army whose
march along the crowded ways of life is marked by monu-
ments of stone and steel pulsating with human life, not
by mute crosses in the poppy fields."

HOME INSURANCE. In Chicago for some forty years
since World's Fair time, at least, there had raged (in a
mild way) a controversy as to the first skyscraper. There
was no question as to its birthplace. That was Chicago—
even New York and St. Louis admitted it—but which was
the first skyscraper in Chicago? There were two claimants.

One the Home Insurance Building, designed by Major Jenney in 1883 and built in 1884, and the other the Tacoma Building built in 1887, Holabird and Roche architects. In these days this author was a member of the Tacoma Building School of Thought [15] and stoutly maintained that though the Home Insurance may have been built some three years earlier it was questionable whether it were of skeleton construction at all, and at most only in small part, while the Tacoma Building we believed was completely skeleton in construction.

A grand opportunity to settle this matter was offered in 1929 when the Tacoma was wrecked and when two years later the Home Insurance met the same fate. To the surprise of both camps it was discovered first that the Home Insurance did in fact employ skeleton construction and far more extensively than had been believed, and secondly that although the Tacoma was of an advanced form of skeleton construction on its two street fronts it was much less so than had been believed in the remainder of the building.

Let us at this point restate the essence of skeleton construction, and let us start with a definition or two. First, a "skyscraper" is a high building of skeleton construction. Second, skeleton construction is a method in which an iron or steel cage (or skeleton) of columns, beams and girders supports all of the remainder of the building. That is, it takes all the loads of floors and walls and carries them down into the ground. Here are two other definitions that we may need. "Party walls" are walls straddling a lot or property line and mutually owned by both owners on either side. "Lot-line walls" are walls abutting a lot line but belonging exclusively to the owner of the lot on which they are built.

[15] See first edition of *The Story of Architecture in America.*

The Home Insurance Building stood on the northeast corner of La Salle and Adams. The resulting L shape had a curious extension like a narrow arm, which extended north from the northeast corner. The foundations were, for the most part, of the isolated stepped stone type, after Baumann's theory, you remember. Along the Adams and La Salle Street fronts solid granite walls arose through two stories. Party walls on the east and north were also of solid masonry, as required by law. All of the rest of the exterior including the court was of skeleton construction of a primitive type, but nonetheless skeleton construction, because the skeleton certainly supported the floors and the walls. The columns were of cast iron, the beams and girders were of wrought iron. Cast iron also were the curious dish-like lintels over the windows and the heavy mullions that ran continuously to the top of the building. Peculiar were the anchor bolts that loosely tied the spandrel girders to the columns and extraordinary were the "cutting lines," as Major Jenney called them, that divided his building into layers every two stories like a gigantic brick and iron cake.

The question at issue is not what Major Jenney intended when he built his crude skeleton of iron but what he accomplished thereby. Frankly, I don't believe he visualized his skeleton as independently supporting the outside facing of the exterior piers, but he knew that most (82%) of the area of the typical pier was supported by his iron frame and that the remainder was so bonded and built in that it was perfectly safe. He was certainly confident that the cast-iron column inside his pier enabled him to reduce its size and get larger windows, hence more light for the offices.

The Home Insurance Building was wrecked in the fall of 1931. The American Metallurgical Society asked the

Field estate, which owned the property, for permission to erect a bronze tablet in the building to be erected stating in effect that the Home Insurance Building was the first skyscraper. They turned to the architects for information, and a committee of architects and others suggested by Ernest R. Graham, architect, including the president of the Chicago Historical Society, president of the Chicago Real Estate Board and a representative of the Museum of Science and Industry, was asked by the Field estate to examine the building in the various stages of its destruction and to determine if possible its claim to primacy, if any. The report of this committee has been printed in book form. Its concluding paragraph, part of which is incorporated in the inscription on the bronze tablet which was erected, is as follows:

"As in the case of every great invention, skeleton construction in its completeness was not, nor could it have been, discovered by any one man nor expressed in any one building. The early buildings for this reason are all more or less transitional and experimental. Each learned from the experience of the preceding and added its contribution in the development of the idea. It is, however, entirely possible, from a consideration of the evidence, to appraise the relative importance of each in terms of its originality and its influence on the work which followed. Acting on this conviction we have no hesitation in stating that the Home Insurance Building was the first high building to utilize as the basic principle of its design the method known as skeleton construction, and that there is convincing evidence that Major Jenney, in solving the particular problems of light and loads appearing in this building, discovered the true application of skeleton construction to the building of high structures and invented and here utilized for the first time its special forms.

From Tallmadge, "Origin of the Skyscraper"

AN OLD VIEW OF THE HOME INSURANCE BUILDING,
JENNEY AND MUNDIE, ARCHITECTS

From the southwest. The two upper floors were added in 1890

From Tallmadge, "Origin of the Skyscraper"

THE HOME INSURANCE BUILDING

Typical pier girdled at the bottom of the spandrel of the third story showing the masonry of the pier above to the top of the building unsupported except for the skeleton frame.

"We are also of the opinion that owing to its priority and its immediate success and renown the Home Insurance Building was in fact the primal influence in the acceptance of skeleton construction; and hence is the true father of the skyscraper."

TACOMA BUILDING. If the examining architects were surprised at the large extent of the iron skeleton in the Home Insurance Building, those who examined the Tacoma Building, wrecked two years earlier, of whom the author was one were equally astonished at the small extent of the skeleton in this building. Although the skeleton extended on the two street fronts from sidewalk to roof and was more perfected in design, having shelf angles designed exclusively for supporting the facings of brick and terra-cotta, yet these two street fronts were the only exterior walls in the building of skeleton construction. The lot line walls, not party walls as in the Home Insurance, could have been skeleton but they were solid, and, most amazing of all, the rear or court walls were also of solid masonry instead of skeleton, where the latter, one would think, would have been the easier construction. Furthermore two great transverse brick walls from foundation to roof ran up through the building, taking their share of the floor loads and bracing the structure.

The great contribution of the Tacoma Building is first its careful study and development of the technique of skeleton construction as applied to the façades of a high building, in which specifically should be mentioned the shelf angle—bolted or riveted to the outside face of the columns and directly supporting the brick and terra cotta facing of the building at each story. Red hot rivets beaten into place held the steel together in the Tacoma Building instead of old-fashioned bolts and nuts. Even here, however, steel had not yet come into its own; the columns were still of cast iron. Wrought iron was used for all special shapes, while steel apparently was used only for the girders and floor beams. Foundations, as usual, called for the most careful study and ingenuity, as the soil was particularly treacherous along La Salle Street. A floating or raft foundation was employed, composed of some twenty inches of concrete in which were embedded steel beams. The floors were of flat tile arches, and the partitions of hollow tile as well. White enameled brick was used in the exterior construction of the courts as had been done in the beautiful court to the Rookery. Every office was lighted with both electricity and gas—the tenant could take his choice!

The plumbing in the Tacoma marked other advances, such as concentration of the toilet-rooms, in this case all the men on the 12th floor and the women on the 11th. Injector pits and pumps kept the basements dry.

Paul Mueller, engineer and builder, told me the idea of skeleton construction in the Tacoma was suggested, not by the Home Insurance Building, but by the Northwestern Terra-Cotta Company, which had worked out a system for supporting terra cotta bays for Adler and Sullivan for the Auditorium, and which were discarded, perhaps owing to the jibe of John Root,[16] but were adopted according to Mueller by Holabird and Roche. At any rate the thirteen-story building was an excellent example of truth and grace—two stories of shops, mostly glass, another story of shops and ten identical stories of offices and an arcaded top. The terra cotta ornament was Romanesque. It was certainly the first architectural recognition of the all-powerful skeleton of steel within. As the

[16] As Root said, "Sullivan couldn't design a building without covering it with ornaments."

walls were practically of glass, divided only by piers and mullions large enough only to provide fireproofing for the steel, we have a new architectural concept. Today we subconsciously allow in eye and mind for the steel skeleton. But it was unknown fifty-one years ago to the man in the street, who must seriously have feared to enter a thirteen-story house built of jackstraws. As much as I admire the taste of Martin Roche in its design, I admire still more the courage of William Holabird in daring to carry it out. As Mark Twain remarked, "After Columbus discovered America it stayed discovered." In that sense the Tacoma was the Columbus of skeleton construction.

CHAMBER OF COMMERCE. One of my earliest thrills was in gazing up in the tremendous interior court of the Chamber of Commerce. It was built in 1889 and was thirteen stories high. Unlike the Rookery, this was roofed with a glass skylight at the top. Two-hundred feet it was above the ground, and an encircling balcony served as hall at each floor. Unfortunately, a clear view was interrupted at the proper intervals by heavy wire screens from wall to wall which were intended to reduce the popularity of this court with would-be suicides. The Chamber of Commerce was razed in 1926 to make way for the Foreman Bank. It stood at the southeast corner of La Salle and Washington where ninety years ago was built the First Baptist Church, seventy-five years ago the first Chamber of Commerce and sixty-seven years ago the first Board of Trade. "In 1888," says Mr. Tapper, engineer and superintendent for the architects Baumann and Huehl, "we put the old Board of Trade Building on screws, took out the old and put in the new foundations." This major operation was followed by building five stories on top of the old walls of the Board of Trade building, making the new Chamber of Commerce thirteen stories in height.

The old entrance can be recognized in the newer building. The style was a rude form of Classic, with a top story evidently inspired by the Rookery. The exterior walls were of solid masonry, according to *Industrial Chicago,* but the *Chicago Tribune* September 13, 1891, says it is of "Chicago construction," that is, skeleton.

MANHATTAN BUILDING. Elmer Jensen, a partner of Major Jenney, the architect of the building, tells me that the Manhattan Building, still standing on the east side of Dearborn between Van Buren and Harrison, was the first skyscraper in which all the walls, fronts, sides and rear are carried on the steel frame. *Industrial Chicago* says much the same thing when it states that the architect used the perfected system known as "Chicago construction" first introduced by him in the Home Insurance building in 1884. The Manhattan is peculiar in that it has two side wings nine stories high and a central shaft sixteen stories high. As it was designed in 1890 and completed in 1891, before the invention of concrete piers down to solid rock, the Major was evidently fearful that what the Auditorium did to the Studebaker (Fine Arts) Building he might do to the eight-story neighbors on each side. But he took an extra precaution and supported the lot line walls with cantilevers, steel arms that stretched out from within—a famous feat of engineering. The style of the Manhattan is Romanesque, with a sequence of 1-2-6-1-3-4-1. A curious relationship, but one of the best buildings the Major did.

The UNITY BUILDING, still standing, was an early skyscraper, as its foundations were laid in May, 1891. It was well known at the time, for it made a record for its speed in construction. It was built with cast-iron columns, which was remarkable, for the building is eighteen stories

high. The superintendent, A. Vanderkloot, made this
statement in the *Inter-Ocean:* "This speed could not
possibly be made if steel columns were used. We used
cast iron, and this is the first iron building constructed
in Chicago with material manufactured at home." Nevertheless, according to *Industrial Chicago,* "Accumulation
of refuse caused the building to sag somewhat but the
perpendicularity was restored." The architect was Clinton
J. Warren, who learned his trade in the office of Burnham
and Root. Beside the Unity he was the architect for the
famous Virginia Hotel that used to stand on the northwest
corner of Ohio and Rush. He built the majority of houses
in Morgan Park, the Church of Our Savior on Fullerton
Avenue, and many stations for both the Burlington and
Rock Island railroads. The Unity Building was a pioneer
in one respect at least and that was the application of
Classic architecture to the skyscraper in the days of the
Romanesque. The Classic style is supposed to have come
in only after the World's Fair set the example, and here is
the Unity looking for all the world as though it had been
hatched in the Court of Honor. The story sequence is
peculiar, 2-9-1-1-1-1-1.

WOMAN'S TEMPLE.   In 1890 the Woman's Christian
Temperance Union was at the height of its power and
fame. Frances Willard, its head, was one of the nation's
most famous personages. What more appropriate than
that this great institution should have a magnificent
monument and at the same time a source of income built
so close to the home of Miss Willard in Evanston and the
birth-place of the Temperance Union? Accordingly the
site at the southwest corner of Monroe and La Salle
streets was secured from Marshall Field. Curiously, this
had been the intended site for the great Wholesale Build-

ing, designed by Richardson. Burnham and Root commenced work on the plans in 1891. The building measured ninety-six feet on Monroe and one hundred ninety feet on La Salle. The thirteen stories rose one hundred ninety-six feet from an H plan, a most unusual plan in those days for a skyscraper. The material was granite for the first two stories and brick and terra cotta above, with a high pitched slate roof—much the same scheme of material as was employed in its contemporary, the Masonic Temple.

It was with real sorrow that we saw the wreckers take possession of the temple that was once the consummated dream of the white ribboners. I thought of Frances Willard, a keen wit herself, flushing at the answer which John Root made to her request for a subject for the mural in the Temple auditorium, "Why don't we paint Christ turning the water into wine?" asked John.

Harriet Monroe writes of the evolution of Root's design, "The first sketches seemed perfunctory, lacked inspiration—a square tall office-building, nothing more." (Perhaps John was not especially sympathetic to the cause.) "Mr. Burnham was the first to view and object. 'If that is honestly your idea of what this building should be, go ahead with it. . . . . But if you are not yet interested, if you have not put your soul into it, try again.' " This sounds so much like Daniel Burnham's "large serious way" which I knew so well, that I quote it as a flash on the great man whom we have had little opportunity, so far, to appraise. In fact, Mr. Burnham suggested the exterior court, one of the first, and perhaps the high roof as well. By this time apparently, "for he made ten or twelve different studies," John threw himself into the task of making the Temple more than an office building.

THE TACOMA BUILDING, HOLABIRD & ROCHE, ARCHITECTS,
BUILT IN 1887

THE MASONIC TEMPLE, BURNHAM AND ROOT, ARCHITECTS

Built in 1891 on northeast corner of State and Randolph streets, now destroyed

The beautiful spire, unhappily never built, was the culmination of his inspiration. Root in the Woman's Temple, feeling probably that the Romanesque was a bit virile for the expression women's aspirations, selected the early form of the French Renaissance as evidenced in some of the royal chateaux of the Loire valley. Beginning with two stories of rugged stone, it becomes more delicate and richer until it culminates in the flowering of the upper stories in dormers and pinnacles. The story sequence which you will observe is gradually approaching the formula of base shaft and cap, against which Sullivan stormed, and which became the bane of the skyscraper after the Fair, is 2-2-5-1-1-2 (roof). In this building, as usual, Root is true to his material, and the moulded brick and flowering terra cotta were among the loveliest in Chicago.

MASONIC TEMPLE. There is no building in Chicago which fired the imagination and enthusiasm, not only of our citizens but of the world, as did the Masonic Temple when it was built in 1891 on the northeast corner of State and Randolph. The cause of its fame was its height. Its twenty-two stories soared two hundred seventy-four feet, not quite threatening the Washington monument as the highest structure in the world, but still astounding the populace. Other important factors in the building were its size, one hundred ninety feet on each street, its cost of $2,000,000, its fourteen elevators (two "express"), its roof garden, and its architects, Burnham and Root. Up to that time the most expensive building in Chicago was the Rookery, which cost 31 cents per cubic foot. The Masonic Temple, however, cost the tremendous sum of 35 cents a cubic foot! The latest, one almost says last, skyscraper, the Marshall Field Office Building built in

1932, cost between 65 and 70 cents per cubic foot. The demands of union labor today have almost killed building construction for private gain, as rents cannot be levied sufficient to make any return on the terrific cost. The construction was of course skeleton steel, accepted now, only six years after the Home Insurance, as the only type for a skyscraper.

The building was stone in its lower three stories, brown pressed brick with terra cotta trimmings for the next thirteen and the remaining four or five of terra cotta culminating in tremendous but graceful gables on the State Street front and a high pitched tile roof. In the design of the building John Root made further advances in his continuous experiments in Americanizing the Romanesque.

Perhaps influenced by the fulminations of Louis Sullivan on form and function, he abandoned his subtle but nevertheless artificial divisions of stories in the Rookery and expressed the uniform purpose of the stories above the street shops by a soaring shaft uninterrupted by horizontal divisions except at the top where a course of arches and the gables occur. I think that he strove here to achieve a "commercial style" based on the Romanesque that might be generally accepted as a formula for the expression of the skyscraper, and he might have prevailed had not the World's Fair almost immediately knocked the hopes of the Romantics into a cocked hat.

Harriet Monroe says John "fretted" over his task in designing the Masonic Temple, that he thought it was too high to begin with, and when another two stories were added while on the draughting-board he was sure of it. While Root attacked the problem in brilliant fashion, in fact establishing the formula for skyscrapers of base, shaft and cap, which was to rule for some thirty years (from 1891 to 1922), yet the building never seemed to be his flesh and blood as did, for instance, the Rookery or the Chicago Club. The sequence of stories in the Masonic Temple shows the new concept for skyscraper façades—Base 2-2—Shaft 12—Cap-1-1 and 2 and more in the roof. No matter what the figures say, the Washington Monument as the highest structure and the Masonic Temple as the highest building held the record so long that they still look it. As I write, this wonder of wonders is being wrecked—having been the observed of all observers for some forty-eight years.

FIREPROOFING

Wight says true fireproofing was introduced in 1880-81, "from which time up to January 1885 there were completed or in process of construction eighteen fireproof buildings costing $100,000 to $1,700,000 each." Nine of these were to be completed simultaneously by May 1, 1885. These nine were the Board of Trade, Home Insurance, Royal Insurance, Opera House block, Gaff, Mallers, Insurance Exchange, Traders, and Parker. All were elevator buildings, except the Home Insurance, the father of the skyscraper. Immediately after, but in the same class, came the Montauk, Pullman, Rookery, Palmer, Marshall Field's store, Traders, Merchants Loan and Trust. The Monadnock is also an elevator building in the sense that it is solid masonry, but as it was built in the era of the skyscrapers with full knowledge of what was going on we must regard it as a freak.

The sudden change in the exterior material of these buildings suggests their revolutionary importance. Whereas in the sixties and the first half of the seventies brick was scorned as inelegant and the façades were built of

Athens marble and galvanized iron or the whole front
of cast iron, in these buildings, pressed brick and terra
cotta have become the style, an eloquent commentary on
the common sense and earnestness of the men of the
eighties. The Royal Insurance had brick for one front
and red granite for the other. The Parker Block had a
brick and sandstone front, and the Board of Trade was
granite on three fronts. Brick buildings were trimmed
with terra cotta, the manufacture of which had made im-
mense strides in Chicago. It will again be noticed that
these materials are all far superior to Athens marble
(Lemont limestone) or to cast iron, both of which are
little better than "fire resisting." It was in the interiors,
however, that fireproof construction much as we know
it today was created. This was before the days of reinforced concrete. Ernest Graham wrote me that, to the
best of his knowledge, no reinforced concrete was used
in the World's Fair of 1893. Concrete was used as a filler
or for slabs that were under no tranverse nor tensile
strains. Fireproofing as developed in the eighties was
based on covering all structural members with some form
of baked hollow clay, which is, of course, terra cotta, or
when used for fireproofing more commonly called tile.[17]
The structural frame of wrought- or cast-iron columns,
girders and beams (there was no steel before 1885) was
completely incased in this hollow tile. The hollow tile was
used as well for floors, either in segmental arches from
beam to beam in the early part of this decade with the
haunches filled in with concrete or later in flat arches.

---

[17] The old form of construction employing segmental arches of brick between iron
beams failed to be fireproof because the lower flanges of the beams were bare and
consequently exposed to the heat of the burning structure; on the other hand the
tile haunch blocks were formed to support a tile slab that covered and protected the
bottom flange of the floor beams and girders.

In the first case the plaster followed the contour of the arch, as there was little metal lath in those days,[18] and in the latter plastered directly on the tile ceiling. The partitions were of structural tile or of terra lumber. Trim and floor surfaces were mostly of wood. One curious anomaly in the class of fireproof building was the approved use of wooden joists. The joists had thin terra-cotta slabs fastened to their undersides and every precaution was taken that there be no openings in the ceiling through which fire could penetrate. P. B. Wight says, in 1885, of this type of construction, "Such a building will resist fire as severe and as long as one in which the I beam and tile arch are used, and there is no reason why it should not be called a fireproof building." He refers to the Insurance Exchange, the Traders and Martin Ryerson's store (Revell Building) as being of this construction. Richard E. Schmidt says the Revell Building at the northeast corner of Wabash and Adams has terra cotta slabs screwed to the bottom of wood joists.

FOUNDATIONS

The matter of "floating foundations," a wide slab of concrete with railroad rails or steel beams imbedded, has been discussed. Their first use in the Montauk Block is perhaps the principal reason for the fame of this building. Here John Root conceived of them at the insistence of Owen Aldis that more room was needed in the basement, for with them the huge pyramidal piles of stone which served as footings were unnecessary. According to Harriet Monroe in the biography of her brother-in-law, they were used as a special device, but their great

---

[18] A patent was taken out in England for wire lath in 1797.

superiority in room-saving, ease of construction, and cost made their acceptance for other tall buildings almost mandatory. And we find them speedily incorporated into the plans for the Rookery, the Rialto and the Phoenix. Miss Monroe states that steel cantilevers were employed for the support of party walls, whereby the weight was shifted from directly beneath the wall to a point within the building, and she intimates that this device was first used in this epochal Montauk. Certainly the principle of the cantilever had been known from antiquity, but it is likely that Root used it for the first time, at least in Chicago, for the support of party walls.

Index

Ada Street Methodist Church, 92
Addams, Jane, 121
Adler, Dankmar, 92, 134, 153, 160, 161, 162, 163
Adler and Sullivan, 153, 154, 155, 156, 157, 161, 187, 198
Adler. *See also* Burling and Adler
Agency House, 22
Aiken Institute, 44
Aiken's Museum, 79
Akron Plan, 172, 173
Alderman, William N., xi
Aldine Square, 119 f., 121
Aldis, Owen, 152, 207
Alexian Brothers' Hospital, 97
Allen, L. F., 34 n.
Altgeld, John P., 191
American architecture, 18, 71 n., 73, 137, 152; Gothic, 122, 167
American Express Company Building, 114
American Gothic architecture, 122, 167
American Institute of Architects, 98, 182
American Merchants Union Express Company, 141
American Metallurgical Society, 195
American Norman Gothic architecture, 146. *See also* Norman architecture
Andersen school, 148
Anderson Press Co., 152, 172
Andreas, A. T., 42 n., 49 n., 57 n., 77, 78, 84, 91, 93, 94, 111, 83 n., 91 n., 96 n., 102 n., 107, 109 n.
Arcade Block, 75
Architectural Iron Works, 109
Architectural literature, 33 f., 47, 70 ff.
Armour Institute of Technology, xi, 183
Armstrong and Egan, 129
Arnold family, 87
Arnold, Isaac N., 51
Art Institute, ix, xi, 33, 90, 167, 184
Ashland Block, 191

"Athens marble," 75, 172, 206. *See also* Stone
Auditorium, 153, 156 ff., 200
Austen Building, 145, 149
Avenue House (Evanston), 74

Badger, A. C., 88
Ballard Block, 115
Balloon construction, 36 ff., 105
Bangley, 129
Bank of Pennsylvania, 33
Baptist Theological Seminary, 98
Barrett, 78
Barry, 71
Basements, 52, 86. *See also* Foundations
Bates, R. W., 185
Battle of the Styles, the, 68, 80
Bauer, August, 96 f., 100, 148
Bauer and Company, 79
Baumann, Edward, 98, 116
Baumann, Frederick, 142, 155, 195
Baumann and Huehl, 199
Baumann. *See also* Burling and Baumann
Beaubien, Jean Baptiste, 25
Beaubien, Mark, 23, 25
Beaubien Land Claim, 25
Bedford Building, 190
Bedford limestone, 172. *See also* Stone
Beman, S. S., 134, 146, 153
Benjamin, Asher, 33, 34 n.
Bibliothèque Ste. Geneviève, 70, 116
Bigelow House, 77, 103
Bishop Foley's Palace, 124
Blair, Mrs. William, 50
Blanchard, 15 n.
Blanchard, Rufus, 84
Blumenthal. *See* Cudell and Blumenthal
Board of Public Works, 103
Board of Trade, 91
Board of Trade Building, 111, 121, 122, 146, 165 ff., 205, 206

Bötticher, 118
Book-Seller Row, 115
Boone Block, 75
Booth, Edwin, 78
Booth, J. Wilkes, 78
Borden Block, 153, 155
Boston Art Museum, 69
Bowen Block, 75, 114
Boyington, William W., 59, 62, 63, 92 f., 94, 95, 96, 98, 100, 112, 116, 121, 122, 131, 151, 166
Brainard, Dr., 87
Brainard school, 148
Brandon, 70 n.
Brattle Street Church (Boston), 138, 141
Bricks, 9, 34, 87, 93, 111, 145, 172, 205 f.
Briggs House, 77
Britton, 70
Brooks, Phillips, 141
Brooks estate, 152
Bross, William, 38, 41
Brown, William "Box," 59
Bryan Block, 75
"Buena House," 87
Building materials, 174, 205 f. See also Bricks; Iron; Lumber; Steel skeleton; Stone; Structural iron work
Burgess, 70, 80
Burling, Edward, 82, 89, 90, 91, 92, 96, 98, 100, 116, 127, 131, 148
Burling and Adler, 129, 131
Burling and Baumann, 55, 62, 63
Burling and Whitehouse, 146
Burlington railroad stations, 201
Burne-Jones, 138
Burnham, Daniel H., 94, 95, 128, 134, 143, 150, 152, 166, 191, 202
Burnham Library, 33, 90, 183
Burnham and Root, x, 135, 142, 145, 147, 149, 153, 165, 166, 167, 178, 181, 190, 191, 201, 202, 203
Butler family, 51
Butterfield, 80
Butterfield, Justin, 51
Byzantine architecture, 111, 112, 123, 139

Cady. See Root and Cady
Cahokia Court House, 4

Caissons, 143, 162, 163, 188. See also Foundations
Caldwell, Billy, 23, 25; home of, 49
Calumet Building, 145 f., 166
Camp Russell, 12 n.
Carcassonne, 70
Carlton, Will, 164
Carpenters and builders, early, 33 f., 37, 47
Carter, Asher, 96
Carter and Bauer, 62, 63
Cathedral of the Holy Name, 55, 59, 81, 104
Cathedral of St. John (New York), 122
Caton, Judge, 30
Cavelier, René Robert, Sieur de La Salle, 2, 3
Centenary Church, 92
Centennial Exposition of 1876, 175
Central Music Hall, 160
Central Union Station, 92, 95
Century of Progress, A, exposition, xii, 6, 13
Chamber of Commerce, 90, 92, 102, 190, 199 f.
Chamberlain, 86 n.
Chambers, 70 n.
Channing, Dr. Walter, 176, 178
Chapman, Cass, 101
Chapman, Charles, 49
Chartres, 173
Chase, Samuel B., 87
Chicago, Burlington and Quincy Depot, 122
Chicago, Burlington and Quincy office building, 151
Chicago Club, 167 f., 205
Chicago Fire, 42, 50, 56, 57, 64, 69, 74, 77, 79, 80, 81 ff., 101 ff., 116 ff., 124 f.
Chicago Historical Society, 6, 14, 104, 196
Chicago Hospital for Women and Children, 97
Chicago Real Estate Board, 196
Chicago River, 11, 27, 28, 54
Chicago Title and Trust Building, 191
Chicago Water Tower, 93, 94 f., 95, 102
Chicagou, 3
Chikago River, 3, 9
Church architecture, xi, 71, 79 f., 139, 171 ff.

Church of the Holy Name, 81
Church of Our Savior, 201
Church Row, 124
City Hall, 62, 102, 124, 166. *See also* Court House
City Hotel, 49
Clark, George Rogers, 10
Clark, Widow, 41, 43, 44
Classic architecture, 75, 76, 80, 85, 90, 111, 113, 115, 118, 119, 122, 142, 146, 180, 181, 189, 201. *See also* Free Classic architecture; Greek Revival
Cleaver, Charles, 37
Cleaverville, 37
Cleveland, S. D., 127
Cliff Dwellers Club, viii
Clybourne family, 23, 41
Clybourne, Archibald, 48
Cobb, Henry Ives, 191
Cobb's Block, 75
"Cobweb Castle," 22
Cochrane, John C., 99
Cochrane and Miller, 129
Cockerell the elder, 33
Colonial architecture, 17 ff., 31, 66, 74, 176. *See also* Post-colonial architecture
Collyer, Robert, 84
Collyer's, Robert, church. *See* Unity Church.
Columbian Exposition (1893), vii, 67, 123, 133, 157, 189, 204, 206
Commercial Gothic architecture, 122. *See also* "Commercial Style" architecture
Commercial Insurance Company, 97
"Commercial Style" architecture, 136, 143, 145. *See also* Commercial Gothic architecture
Concrete, 206
Construction of buildings: of elevator buildings, 136 f., 144 ff., 153, 185; of pioneer dwellings, 4 ff.; of wooden buildings, 33 ff. *See also* Building materials; Fireproofing; Foundations; Skeleton construction
Cook County Abstract and Trust Company Building, 191
Coolidge. *See* Shepley, Rutan and Coolidge.
Couch family, 117
Couch, Ira, 77

Counselman Building, 147 f., 166
County Building, 124. *See also* Court House
County Jail, 125
Court House, 43, 44, 47, 48, 54, 55, 61, 74, 100, 102, 109, 111, 124, 125 ff., 166
Crabtree, Lotta, 78
Cram, Dr., 134
Crane, R. T., 161
Criminal Court Building, 97
Crosby, Uranus H., 78 f.
Crosby's Opera House, 78, 93, 95, 112
Crystal Palace (New York), 68, 70, 96
Cudell, Adolph, 118, 119
Cudell and Blumenthal, 118
Cummings, 72,

Dearborn, General, 11
Dearborn Theatre, 79
Dearborn University, 93
De Jonghe's, 167
Democratic National Convention Hall, 95
Dexter Building, 153, 156
Dickey's Block, 75
Dilettante Society of London, 32
Dixon and Hamilton, 129
Doane, J. W., 99
Domestic architecture, 174 ff.
Donaghue, John, 165
Douglas, Stephen A., 49
Douglas Hall, 95
Downing, A. J., 34 n.
Drake family, 117
Drummond, Mary, 50, 87 n.
Dutton, William, 152

Early American architecture, 18. *See also* American architecture
Early English architecture, 80, 82. *See also* English architecture
Eastlake, Charles, 138
Ecclesiastical architecture, xi. *See also* Church architecture
Ecole des Beaux Arts (Paris), 116, 140
Edbrook, George H., 129
Edbrook, Willoughby J., 99
Eddy, Thomas M., 83 n.
Edelmann, John, 155
Egan, Dr., 47, 48

Egan, J. J., 126, 127. *See also* Armstrong and Egan
Egyptian architecture, 152, 155
Elevator buildings, 136 f., 144 ff., 153, 185. *See also* Skeleton construction
Elizabethan architecture, 180
Emerson, W. R., 176
English architecture, 68, 70, 71, 99, 123, 140, 175, 182; Early, 80, 82; Gothic, 73, 184. *See also* Elizabethan architecture; Queen Anne architecture; Victorian Gothic architecture
Equitable Building, 110
Evanston, Illinois, viii, ix, 86
Exposition Building, 160 f.

Fair Building, 191
Fair Store, 152
Fairbank, N. K., 161
Farwell, Charles B., 181
Farwell, John V., 181
Farwell Block, 93
Farwell Hall, 93
Federal architecture, 19
Federal Building, 75
Fergusson, 70 n.
Field, Henry, 161
Field, Marshall,, 169, 183, 184, 201. *See also under* Marshall Field
Field Wholesale. *See* Marshall Field Wholesale
Fifer, Governor, 160
Fine Arts Building. *See* Studebaker Building
Fireproofing, 106 ff., 109, 110, 143, 188, 205 ff.
First Baptist Church, 27, 57, 92, 199
First Congregational Church of Evanston, xi
First Methodist Church of Evanston, ix, xi
First National Bank, 92, 103, 143, 144, 146
First Presbyterian Church, xi, 14 n., 27, 58, 83, 92
Flanders, John J., 148. *See also* Furst and Flanders
Floating foundations, 155, 189, 198, 207f. *See also* Foundations
Foltz. *See* Treat and Foltz
Foreman Bank, 199

Fort of the pioneer, construction of, 4 ff.
Fort Armstrong, 12 n.
Fort Chartres, 4, 9, 12 n.
Fort Crèvecoeur, 2, 4, 12 n.
Fort Dearborn, 1, 3, 5, 6 ff., 10 ff., 19, 21, 30
Fort Massac, 12 n.
Fort Miami, 3
Fort St. Louis, 2, 12 n.
Foundations, 134, 142 f., 153, 154, 155, 162 f., 185 ff., 189, 198, 199, 200, 207 ff. *See also* Basements
Fourth Presbyterian Church, 60
Framed construction, 35 f.
Free Classic architecture, 122, 139, 177, 190
Freeman, Dr., 57
French architecture, 68, 69, 70, 71, 76, 77, 81, 86, 88, 91, 93, 111, 112, 114, 115, 116, 117, 120, 140; Gothic, 84; Renaissance, 111, 123, 180, 203. *See also* Renaissance architecture
Fuller, Dr. Charles G., 178
Fuller, Henry, 116
Fullerton Block, 75, 115
Furst and Flanders, 101

Gaff Building, 151, 205
Gaillabaud, 70
Gales, 16 n.
Gambrill and Richardson, 141
Garnier, Charles, 120
Garnsey, George O., 99
Garrett's Block, 75
Gay, Henry Lord, 126, 129, 130
Georgian Colonial architecture, 18, 66
German architecture, 77, 140
Glessner, J. J., 142, 182 f.
Goodhue, Bertram, 82
Gothic architecture, xi, 56, 60, 68, 70, 71, 73, 80, 83, 94, 111, 114, 115, 122, 139, 180; American, 122, 167; American Norman, 146; Commercial, 122; English, 73, 184; French, 84; Cathedral, 71; Italian, 73; Mediaeval, 80; Victorian, 73, 80, 91, 93, 137, 141, 142, 167, 171, 176
Gottig, Cord H., 99
Gottschalk, 78
Goudy, W. C., 88
Grace Episcopal Church, xi, 82

Grace Evangelical Lutheran Church of River Forest, xi
Grace Methodist Church, 83
Graham, Ernest R., 196, 206
Grand Pacific Hotel, 76, 77, 93, 96, 103, 109
Grand Union Depot, 93
Granger, Alfred, 182
Grannis Block, 166
"Greek mania," the, 32, 66
Greek Revival, xii, 31 f., 39 f., 42, 44, 46, 49, 51, 52, 54, 56, 58, 64, 66, 73, 74, 75, 79, 84, 85, 89, 90, 111, 112, 116
Greenwich Village, viii
Grey, Charles F., 96
Grover, Frank R., 2 n.

Hack, J. A., 88
Hackett, Karleton, 164
Hale Block, 115
Hall, Emory, 182
Hall and Ayers Block, 117
Hamilton, A. J., 176
Hamilton, F. B., 101. See also Dixon and Hamilton
Hammond, Percy, 164
Harding, George F., 161
"Hardscrabble," 23
Hardy, Guy, 164
Harms, Farmer, 127
Harrison family, 88
Harrison, Carter, 88
Hatfield, R. S., 34 n.
Haven school, 148
Healy school, 148
Herter, Messrs., 185
Hesler, Alexander, 61 f.
Historical American Buildings Survey, xii, 31
Hitchcock, Russell, 69
Hittorf, 70 n., 120
Holabird, John A., xiii, 134
Holabird, William, 199
Holabird and Roche, 190, 194, 198
Holabird and Root, 164
Holly, H. H., 73 f.
Holy Name Cathedral. See Cathedral of the Holy Name
Home Insurance Building, 150, 187, 188, 189, 190, 193 ff., 200, 205

Honoré, Henry H., 88
Honoré Building, 75, 109, 112 f., 115
Honoré Hotel, 115
Hooley's amusement hall, 79
Hoyne school, 148
Hubbard, Gurdon S., 20 f., 22, 26, 47, 48
Hudson River School, 67
Huehl. See Baumann and Huehl
Hunt, Richard M., 69, 116, 141
Hyde Park, 86, 179

Illinois Central Railway, 54, 97, 99, 117
Illinois-Michigan Canal, 31
Indian (East) architecture, 149, 150
Insurance Exchange, 117, 205, 207
International architecture, 65
Iron, for building fronts and roofs, 93, 95 f., 109, 206. See also Structural iron work
Italian architecture, 68, 71, 72, 77, 79, 80, 97, 111, 112, 123; Gothic, 73; Ornament, 122; Palladian, 123; Renaissance, 92; Venetian, 68, 97, 113, 123, 139. See also Renaissance architecture

Jefferson (neighborhood), 179
Jefferson, Joseph, 78
Jefferson, Thomas, 138
Jenney, William Le Baron, 109, 128, 131, 134, 151, 154, 188, 190, 194, 195, 196, 200
Johnson, George H., 109 f.
Joliet, Louis, 31
Joliet limestone, 123, 172. See also Stone
Jones, Bassett, 176
Jones Hall, 95
Joutel, 3
Judd, the Hon. N. B., 88

Karls, Theodore, 127, 129
Kaskaskia, 9
Kendall Building, 110
Kentucky Building, 129
Kenwood, 86, 88
Kerfoot, S. H., 88
Kerfoot, W. D., 116, 118
Kerfoot's Block, 118
Kimball, Fiske, 8 n.
Kimball, W. W., 79
King Block, 115

Kinzie, John, 6, 9, 25, 47, 48; home of, 21 f.
Kinzie, John H., 59; home of, 51
Kinzie, Mrs. John H., 6, 8, 21, 22
Kirkland, Caroline, 25 n., 50 n., 87 n., 88
Krebs, William, 176

Labrouste, 116, 120, 140
La Farge, John, 138
La Framboise (Indian chief), home of, 48
Lake House, 47
Lake Shore and Michigan Southern Railroad Depot, 93, 95, 115
Lake Township, 179
Lake View, 86, 88, 179
Larrabee, C. L., 121
La Salle, de. See Cavelier, René Robert
La Salle Block, 114, 115
Latarouilly, 70
Latrobe, Benjamin, 32, 139
Latrobe, Charles J., 27
Lauthrop, Paul, 161
Lee, Mrs., 182
Lee's farm, 23
Lefèvre, Minard, 34 n., 70, 98
Lefuel, 116
Leiter Building, 187
Lemont limestone. See "Athens marble"
Lenox Library, 69
Leonard, H. Steward, 95 n.
Lewis Cass, Governor, 20
Lewis and Smith, 30 n.
Lincoln, Abraham, 79
Link's Block, 75
Little, Arthur, 176
Log house, construction of, 4 ff.
Lombard architecture, 123
London Guarantee Building, 14, 16
Long, Major, 20
Longhurst. See Tilley, Longhurst and Co.
Loop, the, 134, 189, 192
Lot-line walls, 194
Louisiana Purchase, 10
Louvre, the, 69, 70, 76, 116, 120
Lumber, 15, 27, 34 ff., 38, 175 f.

McCagg family, 51
McCagg, Ezra B., 87
McCarthy's Block, 75

McCormick, Cyrus, 116; home of, 119, 120 f.
McCormick, Mrs. Leander, 52
McCormick Block, 93, 95
McCormick Reaper works, 103
MacIntyre, 33
McKim, Charles F., 139, 176, 179
McLean, Robert, 137
McNeil, William S., 127
MacVeagh family, 142, 183
McVicker, Mary, 78
McVicker's theater, 78, 124
Magie, H. H., 86
Magies' Block, 75
Maison d'Orée, 90
Major Block, 114
Mallers Building, 148, 205
Manhattan Building, 152, 191, 200
Marcott, L., and Company, 120
Marine Hospital, 90
Marquette, Père Jacques, 1 f.
Marshall Field estate, 196
Marshall Field Office Building, 192, 203
Marshall Field Wholesale, 141, 156, 159, 160, 167, 168 ff.
Marshall Field's store, 205
Masonic Hall, 93
Masonic Temple, 190, 191, 202, 203 ff.
Massachusetts Institute of Technology, viii, x
Massasoit House, 93
Matz, Herman, 97, 125
Matz, Otto H., 62, 63, 97, 100, 121, 125, 126, 128, 129, 130, 132
Mediaeval Gothic architecture, 80
Meeker, George B., 87
Merchants Loan and Trust Building, 205
Methodist church, first, 58
Methodist Church of Akron, Ohio, 172
Metropolitan Hall, 79, 93
Michigan Southern Depot, 103
"Mill construction," 187
Miller, 72. See also Cochrane and Miller
Miller, Edgar, ix
Monadnock Block, 151 f., 186, 190, 205
Monroe, Harriet, 152, 165, 202, 204, 207, 208
Montauk Block, 122, 135, 142, 143 f., 166, 205, 207, 208

Moody Institute, 83
Moore, Judge Samuel M., 88
Moorish architecture, 180, 184
Morgan, Moses, 14
Morgan Park, 201
Morris, William, 183
Morrison, Hugh, 155 n., 160, 162 n., 163 n.
Mueller, Paul, 159, 198
Mullen, 170
Mundie, William B., 191
Municipal Building, 126
Murdoch, actor, 78
Murdock, C. H., 129, 131
Museum of Science and Industry, 196
Musham, H. A, 14 n.

Nash, 70
Nash, Henry H., 107 f.
Néo-Grec, 32, 116
Nesfield, 177
Newberry, Julia, 87
Newberry, Walter N., 87
Newberry Library, 87
New England Church (Congregational), 82, 104
Nicholson, Peter, 34 n. See also Olmstead and Nicholson
Nixon, W. P., 161
Nixon Building, 96, 97, 115
Norman architecture, 83, 112, 140. See also American Norman Gothic architecture
North Presbyterian Church, 60, 92
Northern Hotel, 190
Northwest Side, 179
Northwestern Terra-Cotta Company, 198
Norton, William, 48
Nouvelle Opéra, 120

Oakley, Horace, 168
Odd Fellows, 191
Office-buildings, 144. See also Elevator buildings
Ogden family, 51
Ogden, Mahlon D., 131; home of, 86
Ogden, William B., 90; home of, 41, 45, 46, 49, 50, 52, 89, 106
Ohio Wesleyan University, x, xi
Old Iron Block, 96

Olmstead and Nicholson, 63. See also Van Osdel and Olmstead
Opera House, 124, 205
Orchestra Hall, x
Oriental Building, 117
Orphan Asylum (Catholic), 104
Otis Block, 75, 114
Ouilmette, Antoine, 9, 15, 22, 26
Owings Building, 190
Owsley, John E., 88

Paderewski, 183
Palladian Italian architecture, 123
Palladio, 70 n.
Palmer, C. M., 101, 113
Palmer, Frank W., 88
Palmer, Potter, 120, 184 f.
Palmer, Mrs. Potter, I, 88
Palmer, Potter, Building, 109, 205
Palmer House, 47, 76, 77, 96, 103, 113, 114, 116, 117, 135
Paris Opera House, 69, 70, 72, 120
Parker Block, 205, 206
Parrish, Randall, 12 n.
Party walls, 194
Parvenu architecture, xii, 40, 46, 66, 67, 72, 85, 121, 128, 135, 166, 180
Patterson, Robert W., 56
Patti, Adelina, 160
Pavilion Richelieu, 120
Pearson, J. L., 71
Peck, Ferdinand, 160, 161
Peck, P. F. W., 49
Pegged construction, 36
Periolat's (Clem) Bean Club, 127
Perkins Astronomical Observatory, x, xi
Pettle, 9
Phoenix Building, 149, 208
Pierrefonds, 70
Pinet, Père Pierre, 2 f.
Pittsburgh Jail, 169
Plate glass, 145
Plymouth Church, 83
Point Sable, Jean Baptiste, 9, 21
Porches, 13, 17, 41, 86
Porter, Jeremiah, 58, 83
Porticos, 34, 39
Portland Block, 75, 114, 122

Post-colonial architecture, 18, 19, 33, 46, 66
Potter, W. A., 183
Prefabrication, 37
Presbyterian Church of Lake Forest, 57
Prettyman, William, 183
Price, Bruce, 175, 176
Pugin, Augustus A. W., 68, 70, 71
Pullman, Town of, 122
Pullman, George M., 183
Pullman Building, 146 f., 155, 166, 186, 205
Purple Block, 76

Quaife, M. M., 3, 21
Queen Anne architecture, 122, 136, 137, 139, 146, 175, 176, 177, 178, 179, 180, 181, 182, 190

Raguenet, 145
Randall, S. P., 129
Ream, Norman, 183
Reaper Block, 117
Renaissance architecture, 68, 76. See also French architecture; Renaissance; Italian architecture; Renaissance
Renwick, James, 69
Repton, 70 n.
Revell Building, 153, 155, 207
Revett, Nicholas, 32, 33, 118
Rialto Building, 145, 149, 208
Richardson, Henry Hobson, 69, 70, 121, 128, 135 ff., 139, 140 f., 142, 145, 155, 156, 157, 159, 168, 169, 170, 171, 178, 179, 182, 185. See also Gambrill and Richardson
Ricker, Professor, 182
Rickman, 70 n.
Riddle, John, 73
Ripon College, xi
Robinson, half-breed, 15
Robinson, Chief, 23
Roche, Martin, 199. See also Holabird and Roche
Rock Island Depot, 103
Rock Island railroad stations, 201
Rockefeller Center, 193
Rockwell, J., 53
Rogers, Judge J. S., 88
Rogers Groups, 67

Romanesque architecture, 33, 40, 42, 46, 60, 75, 111, 112, 121 f., 128, 133 ff., 139 ff., 145, 146, 149, 157, 158, 159, 166, 167, 168, 169, 171, 173, 175, 178, 179 f., 181, 190, 204
Rookery, the, 145, 149 ff., 186, 190, 198, 203, 204, 205, 208
Root, John, 37, 70, 134, 143, 145, 147, 148, 150, 151, 152, 154, 155, 159, 165, 168, 171, 174, 180, 182, 186, 198, 202, 203, 204, 207, 208
Root and Cady, 79
Root. See also Burnham and Root; Holabird and Root
Rose, Rufus, 129
Rosehill Cemetery Gate, 95
Ross. See York and Ross
Royal Insurance Building, 151, 205, 206
Roycemore School, Evanston, xi
Rumsey family, homes of, 87
Rumsey, George F., 86
Rush Medical College, 104
Ruskin, John, 68, 70, 80
Ruskin architecture, 68, 72, 73, 80, 114
Rutan. See Shepley, Rutan and Coolidge
Ryerson, Anne, 51
Ryerson, Joseph T., xiii
Ryerson, Joseph T., 50, 51, 52
Ryerson, Martin, 207
Ryerson Building, 153, 154, 156, 157

St Clair, Arthur, 10
St. James' Episcopal Church, 48, 59, 60, 81, 91, 104
St. James' Methodist Church, xi
St. Joseph's Church (German; Catholic), 104
St. Mary's Roman Catholic Church, 56, 57, 124
St. Patrick's Cathedral (New York), 69
St. Paul's Universalist Church, 84, 92, 95
St. Stephen's Church, old, 81
Ste. Geneviève, Library of. See Bibliothèque Ste. Geneviève
Saloon Building, 49
Sammichele, 113
Sauganash Hotel, 23, 27
Saugatuck, Michigan, ix
Sauvageot, 70
Scammon, J. Y., 95

Scammon Block, 75
Schmidt, Richard E., 99, 118, 141, 207
Schoolcraft, Henry R., 20
Schumann Heink, 183
Schuttler, Peter, 89
Scott, Gilbert, 70, 71, 80
Second Baptist Church, 43
Second Presbyterian Church, 56, 57, 83, 96, 109, 124
Sexton, P. J., 127
Seymour, Ralph Fletcher, xiii
Shaw, Edward, 34 n.
Shaw, Norman, 138, 176, 177, 182
Sheahan, James W., 123
Sheldon family, 51
Sheldon, 184
Shepley, Rutan and Coolidge, 142, 183
Sherman, F. C., 49
Sherman House, 76, 77, 93, 95, 96
Shipman, S. V., 151
Sisters of Mercy, the, convent for, 124
Skeleton construction, 109, 152, 185 ff. See also Elevator buildings; Skyscrapers; Steel skeleton; Structural iron work
Skyscrapers, 145, 152, 186, 189, 190, 192 ff., 196 f., 201, 203, 205. See also Skeleton construction
Smith, A. J., 100
Smith, E. Willard, 62, 63
Smith, Marie Roget, 121
Smith, Perry H., 119
Smith, H. J. See Lewis and Smith
Snow, G. W., 38, 39
Spanish architecture, 140
Spiked construction, 36
Sprague, A. A., 161
Stanton, George, E., 87
State Bank of Illinois, 49
State House, Springfield, Illinois, 99
Steel skeleton, 190, 191, 198, 199, 200. See also Structural iron work
Stockton, General Joseph, 87
Stone, 92
Stone, 9, 34, 74, 80, 93, 122, 123, 124, 127, 171 f., 174, 205 f. See also "Athens marble"
Stoughton, Mrs. M. F., 176, 178
Street, George Edmund, 70, 81

Structural iron work, 107 f., 109, 188, 191, 198, 200 f. See also Iron; Skeleton construction; Steel skeleton
Stuart, James, 32, 33, 118
Studebaker Building, 153, 200
Sturges elevator, 97
Sturgis, architect, 131
Sullivan, Louis, 92, 134, 137, 139, 143, 147, 153, 154, 155, 156, 157, 158, 159, 160, 161, 162, 164, 170, 198 n., 203, 204. See also Adler and Sullivan
Summer School of Painting at Saugatuck, Michigan, ix
Swearingen, Lieutenant, 11

Tabernacle Baptist Church, 58
Tacoma Building, 144, 190, 194, 197 ff.
Tallmadge, Thomas Eddy, vii-xiii, 45 n., 82
Tallmadge and Watson, ix, x
Tapper, 199
Taylor, August D., 56
Taylor, Bert Leston, 164
Temple Building, 57
Terra cotta, 172, 198, 206, 207. See also Fireproofing
Terrace Row, 117, 124
Third National Bank, 115
Thomas, C. P., 99, 100
Thomas, Theodore, 79
Thomas, William, 99
Thomas. See also Wheelock and Thomas
"Tiffany windows," 173
Tile, 206 f. See also Fireproofing
Tilley, Thomas, 126 f., 130
Tilley, Longhurst and Co., 129
Traders Building, 205, 207
Transportation Building, 155, 157
Treat and Foltz, 181
Treaty of Greenville, 3, 10
Treaty of Paris of 1783, 10
Tree, Mrs. Lambert, 86
Tree Studio Building, 86
Tremont House, 27, 76, 77 f., 90, 96, 97, 111, 114
Tribune Building, 92
Trinity Church (Boston), 121, 136, 138, 140, 141, 173
Trinity Church (Methodist), 83
Troescher Building, 153, 155, 157, 187

Tuley, Judge Murray F., 88
Tuscan architecture, 139

Uhlich Block, 76
Union Block, 75
United States Customs House, 107, 123
United States Depository, 107, 124
United States Post-Office, 27, 83, 107, 123
Unity Building, 191, 200 f.
Unity Church, 84, 104
Universalist Church, 95
University of Chicago, the old, 93, 95, 98
University of Chicago Observatory, 95
University of Texas, xi
Upton, George P., 123

Vanderkloot, A., 201
Van Osdel, J. M., 38, 44 ff., 48, 49, 50, 55, 56, 60, 61, 63, 74, 78, 89, 96, 98, 99, 105, 109, 113, 117, 124,
Van Osdel and Olmstead, 63, 124
Van Rensselaer, Mrs. Schuyler, 138, 140, 141
Venetian architecture, 68, 97, 113, 123, 139
Victorian Gothic architecture, 73, 80, 91, 93, 137, 141, 142, 167, 171, 176
Viollet-le-Duc, 70
Virginia Hotel, 52, 201
Visconti, 116
Vitruvius, 70 n.

Wabash Avenue Methodist Church, the, 83, 92
Wadskier, T. V., 99, 148
Wahl, Louis, 161
Walker Warehouse, 156
Waller, Edward, 150
Waller, Henry, 89
Waller, James B., 87
Walsh, John R., 161
Ward, Jasper D., 89

Ward, Mrs. Joseph E., 25 n.
Ware, Robert, 69
Warren, Clinton J., 191, 201
Washington Heights, 179
Washington Monument, 203, 205
Watson, Vernon S., ix, x. See also Tallmadge and Watson
Wayne, General Anthony, 10
Webster, Henry Kitchell, 164
Welsh, L. C., 129
Wentworth, Elijah, 23
Wentworth, John, 16
Wentworth, Long John, 25, 62
West, Charles, xiii
Western Union Building, 149
Wheelock family (of architects), 97 f.
Wheelock, A. L., 100
Wheelock and Thomas, 129
Whistler, Captain John, 11 ff., 21
Whitehouse, Bishop, 81
Whitehouse. See Burling and Whitehouse
Wight, P. B., 141, 207
Willard, Frances, 201, 202
Williams, Eli B., 90
Williamsburg, Virginia, xii
Wilmette, Illinois, 22
Windett Building, 115
Wing, J. M., 98 n.
Wolcott, Dr. Alexander, 22
Wolf Tavern, 76
Woltersdoff, Arthur, 141, 182
Woman's Christian Temperance Union, 201
Woman's Temple, 190, 191, 201 ff.
Wood's Museum, 79
World's Fair of 1893. See Columbian Exposition
Wrenn Library, xi
Wright, Frank Lloyd, 151

York and Ross, 129